From

MALCOLM.

If I found myself on a Journey
with Dwight. This book is a

A Season of Big Mountains

Master PIÈCÉ

Dwight Marshalleck

A time to keep silence and a time to speak.

-Ecclesiastes 3:7-

© 2017 Dwight Marshalleck

ISBN 13: 9781540547958

ISBN-10: 1540547957

Disclaimer
This story is entirely fictional. Characters, names, places, and events are wholly from the author's imagination. Any resemblance to persons, living, or dead is completely coincidental.

It's not the same day a leaf drop inna water, that it rots.

-Jamaica Proverb-

Dedication

To my mother and father. Though you were complete opposites, I tried to balance your fortes instead of your flaws.

It is the first drink that gets you drunk.
-Al-Anon-

Acknowledgement

I could not have written this book without the help of several people. Thank you to my friend, Dr. Richard Birchwood, who helped me mold my first draft into a story. My sincere gratitude to my family for giving me the space to indulge in the lonely art.

I am indebted to my writing group, the Ink Bloods; especially Sue, who read this book three times. Also, Pat for all her encouragement and Joe, my friend and mentor, thank you for pushing me to "write it better."

A heartfelt thank you to all my friends who inspired me along the journey. Lastly, I am thankful to my editor, Candy Johnson, for her thorough revisions.

Part 1: Myths of the Cedar Trees.

Chapter 1

At the top of the twisted, rock-strewn path, bits and pieces from my nightmares lurked behind the door of the pit-latrine. I clambered up the stone steps, nudged the creaky cedarwood door, and peered inside. The musty floorboards overflowed with memories of my foreparents who once thumped across the warped, hollow flooring. A waist-high wooden box on the dimly lit floor seemed more like a coffin than a toilet seat. Sheepishly, I raised the lid and gaped into the dark pit below. It opened all the way to hell. I wondered how anyone plucked up enough courage to perch above that hole and still find peace.

Mamma had no luck potty training me. Normally a patient mother, she desperately wanted me trained so I could leave for the preschool next door. Earlier, she let slip that a black scorpion stung Father's arse one night as he sat on the latrine seat. My indestructible father vomited up his guts and almost died from the scorpion's venom.

I dreaded the strange insects that roamed below the toilet seat, wiggling long antennae up at me. Armor-plated cockroaches, self-assured rulers of the under-seat world, ducked in and out of the shadows. To put me at ease, Mamma lit a sheet of newspaper and chased them back to where they came from, no less a place than hell.

She promised I would be safe during the day since scorpions were creatures of the night. I believed her, but my fear choked back her attempts to get me to settle down on the toilet seat. I hopped down the steps and ran. She followed, imploring.

"Try Dan-Dan, try. You want me tell the health inspector you won't go to the toilet?"

Everyone in the community remained on alert for the public health inspector's visit. From the dread in her voice, I guessed that the man despised little boys who feared the pit-toilet.

"No, nuh, Ma. Do, nuh tell pon me."

I wanted to overcome my fear and make Mamma happy. She had enough trouble appeasing Father's fickle moods.

Below our house, a donkey's bold bray bounced off the hillsides and filled our valley with echoes. The youngster, teetering on the barebacked donkey, called out to Mamma.

"The sanitary inspector man a come."

"Him soon come?"

"Nuh. Him at the crossroad."

A come was imminent. *Soon come* may never come. The donkey trotted away. Local legend says a donkey brings hasty news. Over hills and gullies, the surefooted trot of a donkey is faster than the lumbering gait of man or woman.

Two weeks previously, the Ministry of Health sent a bulletin to the tiny post office by the crossroad. The aloof postmistress gummed the notice to the coarse stucco wall and retreated behind the single window of her office. Onlookers stared at the bulletin and a few, literate enough, mumbled aloud.

"Door-to-door inspection of latrines north-west along Foga Road."

The inspector would see our brightly painted house clinging to the hillside above Foga Road. He may well condemn our latrine unless it looked sturdy, spotless, and sanitary. The owner of a condemned outhouse disgraced the community, and neighbors made up songs to shame the family. Shame wore many faces in our village and showed up frequently to keep folks in their place.

As the health inspector arrived, I waited with Mamma by the kitchen door listening to the noontime news on our transistor radio. She clicked it off to save the batteries. Her eyes, red from the kitchen smoke, smiled at the officer. Her welcome disappointed me. The stranger was the enemy.

Razor-sharp creases on his linen shirt cut a line keener than the seams of his freshly ironed khaki pants. His dark skin glistened as brightly as his penetrating eyes. Clean-shaven, he did not have the stubble that Father sprouted until his weekly trim on Saturdays. The inspector grinned flawless teeth as he tried to coax me out from behind Mamma's skirt. I pulled away, guarding my potty secrets.

"I am here to ensure that you are maintaining the proper hygiene ..."

Nobody spoke with such perfect diction in my community. The voice requested, instead of commanding Mamma to expose our most private affairs.

I held my breath. Would Mamma disclose my potty secrets to the inspector? Would I bring disgrace to my family?

Instead, she chatted with him before pointing to the outhouse. The man studied the structure. It stood sturdy, clean, and a safe distance from the kitchen. The insects stayed out of sight as he finished his checklist. Our latrine passed the test.

Beaming, he turned to me and questioned, "Now, who will walk me to the gate?"

I wondered why the stranger bothered to engage a barefooted boy leaning against a kitchen blackened by the soot of countless mealtime fires. Normally adults commanded children with grunts and broken sentences.

"Lil children should be seen and not heard," an uncle once said.

I struggled to find the language and rise to the level of this educated man. No words in our Patois could match his eloquence. A long pause heightened my unease, but Mamma refused to speak on my behalf. A hint of a smile twinkled in her eyes. I squirmed.

In place of my usual "me nuh know sah" dialect, another voice popped out of my mouth.

"I don't know if I can do that, sir."

The sound of my voice surprised me. I had copied the delivery of the cultured man. As the words flowed off my lips, I came out of hiding and faced his stare.

The smile slid off his face. His eyes swept me over, searching for more. He turned to Mama and pinned her with his gaze.

"Try with him. He will go far."

Mamma's face lit up. Her fingers ran through my hair, untangling the coils, but just as quickly the knots tightened back around her fingers. Tingling all over, I nestled closer.

Together we watched the man navigate the rocky path down to the road below our house. I fought the uneasy feeling that he spotted something about me that foretold an unusual future. Perhaps sensing we were watching, he glanced back and waved.

Long after the visitor left with his smile, Mamma held on to me. She smelled like vanilla from the sweet potato pudding slowly baking on the charcoal fire. I closed my eyes, pondering how far life might take me, but if I posed a question to grownups, I might well get the "Wait till you are twenty-one," reprimand.

Going far in life might be too strange a journey. I never ventured outside my quiet valley, but often I heard the wind blustering though the surrounding hills. Beyond my mountain horizon were other mountains, and what else I wondered. When Mamma let me go, I glanced up at her face. Her eyes were far way, dreaming.

The next time I felt the urge to go to the toilet, I fought back the fear of the insects crawling beneath the wooden seat, crouched gingerly, and grimaced. Mamma stopped threatening to report me to the inspector, but she often reminded me of his appeal.

Try with him. He will go far.

Chapter 2

In the last hour before dawn, a thousand bullfrogs ceased their nightlong mating calls, and the echoes of their croaks merged into the hills. Peenie Wallies, the ever-present fireflies, gave a final wink before the dark devoured them. Bats plunged into caves. Crickets lost their chirps, and all nocturnal creatures fled before first light.

A screech owl's eerie call from the heavens shattered the peace over the mountains. Ol' folks said the bird carried a message. Somewhere within the sound of this ghostly cry, a mother was giving birth. Her wail and the cry of the bird were one. Six years ago, my Mamma heard the same owl's call before I tumbled into the waiting arms of the local midwife.

As the screeches faded, the bird, a mere silhouette against the stars, flapped silently, and flitted to escape the approaching light.

Mornings were the only time of day that Father seemed free of his troubles. Before daybreak, he leapt out of bed to welcome dawn into the valley. Owl calls meant nothing to him, but the pink wisps of clouds in the East drove him to jump up and prepare for a hard day in the fields.

"Red cloud a cut," he announced as if swinging his machete through the heart of a banana tree to reap its fruits. Father loved his machete as much as he cherished the harvest.

I feigned sleep as long as possible. Father shaved kindling for the outdoor kitchen. As he lit the flames, the smell of burning wood drifted into the bedroom. Soon the aroma of roasting coffee beans filled the air and beckoned me to the kitchen. I stayed in bed and listened.

Father turned the handle on the coffee machine as he crushed the roasted beans. I heard tap-tap as he tapped the coffee grounds in a drip bag that Mamma had sewn from an empty cotton flour sack. Next, Father poured hot water into the bag, and the brew tinkled down into the huge, white enamel mug on the kitchen table.

My three siblings were playing the same game, pretending to be asleep. I clung to my innocent childhood dreams.

When we rose at Mamma's prompting, Father had long gone to the fields, and I'd missed the short-lived period before the sun poked over the mountains and into the valley. That suited me fine. I preferred Mamma's nurturing ways of doing most things.

"Hmm, your daddy's coffee is too strong," she warned, and so she made the children's drink foamy and diluted with goat's milk.

Mamma always prepared some culinary delight to compliment the coffee. She made pastries appear out of anything that possessed the smallest hint of food value. A couple of eggs from the fowl coop, a grated coconut, flour and spices, and the soot-covered kitchen soon smelled like heaven.

If her chicken did not lay eggs, she roasted yams or sweet potatoes on the charcoal fire. Slices of freshly roasted sweet potatoes were my favorite way to begin the morning.

After breakfast, my two older sisters left for the elementary school. The youngest sibling, a four-year-old boy, followed Mamma like a shadow. I felt too sick to go to the school, so I crawled back to bed.

"Looks like he won't be with us long,"

Mamma voiced quietly from outside. Why was Father home early from the fields? He grunted before replying.

"Boy's pure skin 'n bones, skin 'n bones to rass." Father often echoed his own words for emphasis.

I slid down from the bed and peeked out, so they would stop talking about me. I felt sickly, but they needed to see that I was still alive. Mamma caught me staring through the door and shushed Father silent.

Next day, Father placed me on the donkey and headed to the doctor for my first trip out of the valley. The smell of the pack material on the jenny-ass reminded me that I had helped Father weave the padding from the midribs of dried banana leaves. He made me hold one end of the material while he twisted the other into a twine. Next, he wrapped the twine into a small rectangle and sewed it with his long, black pack needle. Little by little, he sewed on more twine until he'd stitched enough padding to cover the donkey's back.

Father held a steady hand on the lead rope and marched quickly ahead of the donkey. We used the back roads. Father could hire the car that belonged to his brother Buster to take us to the doctor in town, but the brothers despised each other. An ancient quarrel over rights to family land left a great rift in our family.

We traveled for miles up the hills to a clinic in a little township called Mountain. Father knew about a legendary Chinese doctor who, once a week, saw patients at the clinic. Chinese doctors cured any illness. The doctor saved a boy on his deathbed from dysentery. Everyone fondly called him the "Chiney" doctor.

The town of Mountain stretched up and down paved roads on the hillside. Tiny shops dotted the wayside. The farmers' market at the center of town remained closed on weekdays.

Father guided the jenny-ass down a cobblestone roadway to the sky-blue building housing the clinic. Pebbles crunched as a minibus bustled past us to the health center. Father's hand tightened on the rope to steady the animal.

A woman hoisted two children out of the van and pulled them up the steps to the clinic. Father tied the jenny-ass to a breadfruit tree beside the doctor's office and then lifted me down. We were the only family to ride a donkey to the clinic.

He marched me into the health center and disregarded the wails that filled the air. Children cried as the nurse dragged them back to get their injections. Others wept when they heard agonized screams behind the doctor's door.

Amidst the tears, the choking smell of sterilizing alcohol permeated the room. Fear and pain laid in wait whenever I smelled alcohol.

I felt superior to these weeping children. My father's blood ran through my veins. I could never show weakness by howling with them. At six years old, I tried to be hard and unfeeling as my father.

Soon, the doctor's assistant called us back to see the Chiney doctor. I traced the smell of alcohol to a white, enamel pan filled with menacing hypodermic needles. The doctor gave no diagnosis. He simply laid me across his lap and exposed my backside. In terror, I glanced over my shoulder as he seized a sharp needle from the pan and fitted it to a giant syringe. The needle pierced my posterior like a red, hot awl. I thought of the scorpion stinging my father in the arse as he sat on the toilet seat. I did not flinch.

The Chiney doctor beamed and turned to Father.

"First class," he proclaimed, as if he shared some proud milestone with my pain. How many children cried on his lap?

Father stood straight and stoic. A few of the spider web of worry lines slid off his face, and his eyes softened as he smiled. I knew the doctor couldn't spot the change. Years spent working outdoors in the sun fixed Father's face into a leathery grimace.

"Come, Dan-Dan."

His normally harsh voice hushed to a whisper as he helped me with my trousers. I'd just made my father proud.

"Pull up you trouziz."

"Yes, Papa."

We reserved "Papa" for rare, tender moments in our family. I had found the way to my father's secret, softer side.

Chapter 3

"Patient man ride donkey," ol' folks used to say. An impatient man, Father's donkey must be hard working and long-suffering. The animal waited quietly where we left her next to a row of croton bushes. Father tightened the girth and helped me mount up for the ride home.

Halfway down the first hill, we stopped at a grocery shop. The shopkeeper's face towered above the dark hardwood counter. A slow smile crept across his face.

"Uncle Gil," he called out affectionately. People who liked Father called him Uncle.

I had never heard of this man who greeted us with such warmth. I withheld my question. Father had no patience for abstract questions.

I wished I could tell the man about my "first class" award from the doctor's office, but little boys kept quiet around grown men. These men were different from the self-assured health inspector who encouraged me to speak up.

Father pointed to the thick, keloid welts snaking across the shopkeeper's arm.

"What happened to you hand?"

The man explained that he tackled a machete-wielding burglar who broke into his shop. The culprit chopped him several times and took his money.

"Thank God fe Jesus. I am still in de land of de living."

Why should the scarred shopkeeper be so grateful? A man so wronged should show more anger at his assailant.

In the back of the shop, a tall man propped himself against the hardwood counter and watched. He leaned like a tree half-blown over by the last hurricane and stayed that way, growing sideways. His elbows were blunt daggers poking through the worn sleeves of his khaki shirt. The touch of his arm marked off the years and polished the counter to a shiny hue. When I peered at the man, he dropped his eyes to the concrete floor as if he'd lost his shadow there.

"What you want? I'll buy you anything." Father motioned toward the pastries in the glass case. I jumped at the rare opportunity to get my favorite treat.

"Papa." I pointed to the ginger bun topped with a wedge of cheese. He nodded and added a Kola champagne soda. The drink's bright golden glow offered to soothe the ache from the injection. He bought nothing for himself, since he rarely ate away from home.

As we left the little shop, rain clouds turned the skies gray as twilight in a narrow valley. Father lifted me back onto the packsaddle. The man from the back of the shop shifted just enough to see us depart. Through the haze, I felt him glaring at us, the curious threesome: man, donkey, and a meager boy with a big head.

Rain poured from the sky. Father wrapped me in his raincoat. He had purchased the garment in America decades earlier, when he worked in a factory in Cleveland, Ohio. He had good reason to protect me from the downpour. An older cousin got a "bad injection" from the doctor and walked out in the rain. He swelled up and died shortly after.

Father again took the halter and charged ahead of the donkey. The sound of his boots striking the ground marked his relentless pace. Through an opening in the raincoat, I watched his broad shoulders. He pulled his felt hat down on his head, and rainwater streamed off the brim. He stared dead ahead into the deluge.

He did not break his intense focus to speak to me. I was awed at the stamina of my sixty-six-year-old father. Every step the donkey took hurt my injection site, but I swallowed the pain and steeled myself to match Father's toughness. I clung to the swaying packsaddle.

As the miles passed, I nibbled on the spice bun. I moaned as the packsaddle rocked back and forth jarring my sore bottom. The crunch of loose pebbles under Father's feet hammered a tempo in my head. I dozed off and dropped my favorite soda, unfinished, in the hamper next to me.

The rain trickled to a stop as we climbed the last hill before home. I opened the raincoat and peered out. Clouds still clung to the skies across the hills and a grey mist hung in the air. Dusk had come early to our valley.

Children from the elementary school hurried past, their tiny bare feet flipping aside pebbles in their haste. Normally they dilly-dallied, stretching the evening into hours of leisure. No electric power lines ran up to our area, and everybody rushed home before dark. Unknown entities haunted the nights.

After an eternity, the pebbles stopped tracing their footfalls. The packsaddle ceased swaying. We were home.

Father lifted me down. He whisked the packsaddle from the donkey, guided the animal over to the pasture, and set her loose. Free of her burden, she shook her entire skin and galloped away. Her hooves thundered on the red, wet soil.

She seemed happy to be back. Normally donkeys hated to work in the rain and might lay down with a load still strapped to their backs. Only Father's skill pressed her to labor so hard to bring me home.

Mamma walked from the kitchen where her cooking duties kept her chained to the fireside. Her soft, brown features melted into a knowing smile. Perhaps she knew, intuitively, that the trip strengthened the bond between father and son.

"Tek him, Miss Ena," Father grumbled at her. The edge returned to his voice. He should be more patient with Mamma. She carried me off.

Outside, night edged into the village and darkened the bottom of the hills. Shadows stole up the side of the slopes and stripped the dim glow from the surrounding peaks. Night draped everything motionless until morning. Soon the frogs' croaks would again fill the valley.

I slept for a long time, and when I awoke, my sickness had passed. Either the Chiney doctor's medicines cured me, or the long march with my father steeled me to shake off whatever ailed me.

Chapter 4

Our dog, Rally, joined the family before my birth. As a toddler, I first recalled his howl echoing the wails of my baby brother, Serge. Rally seemed to be in more agony than Serge and I ambled over to check on the dog. I was used to my brother's cry. In time, I learned to ignore Rally's sympathy whimper.

Father taught Rally and the other dog, Castro, to chase off the mongooses from our yard. Mongooses were the biggest pests to a farmer's chicken coop. Clever hunters, mongooses preyed on chicken and looted the hen house for eggs.

When hunting, Rally's powerful bark summoned the neighbors' dogs to join him in the hunt. All the men along the hillside ran with their dogs to the chase, but one neighbor, Isaiah, refused to join the hunt. The man kept to himself.

The other neighbors celebrated Rally's skill at tracking and catching mongooses. As the village's best mongoose dog, everyone welcomed him on their lands, but Rally seemed afraid to venture on Isaiah's property.

Perhaps Rally sensed the disturbing stillness shrouding the man's house. Large "saw-back" green lizards lived on the cedar trees next to his gate. Nobody knew why the lizards suddenly appeared, and stories circulated that they were ghosts guarding the cedar trees.

My father knew how to flush mongooses from their hideouts in the rock walls. He placed a dog on either side of the wall and positioned Rally on top of the rock pile. Next, he shoved an iron bar into the wall and rattled to drive the mongoose in the direction of the dogs. The quarry poked out its head, flared sharp teeth, and scurried for a safer location. Rally pounced on the fleeing prey.

In a fury of snarls and flashing teeth, the pack of dogs celebrated their kill. Rally held the victim's head in his mouth, and Castro pulled the hindquarters until they ripped the prey in two. The lower-ranked dogs tried to join in the kill, but the brutal carnage ended too quickly. Father warned us to keep our distance in the melee lest, during these moments of primal passion, Rally and Castro forget their roles as protectors and turn their fangs on us.

When they finished shredding the animal, the dogs pounced on each other for a fight. Father walked among their bared teeth with his knee-high rubber boots. He placed the iron bar between them and shouted something in a language that the dogs understood. Surprisingly, the melee subsided, the dogs plopped down, panting, and licking the blood from their faces. Then it was safe to call home.

"Come Rally."

If Rally followed us away from home, our neighbors kept their hands off us when the protective hound circled nearby. As I walked down to the road below our house one day, a man ambled up to us. He heaped praises on my younger brother, Serge, and compared his good looks to our deceased grandfather, Ol' Joe. When the man touched my brother, Rally rushed to protect us.

Incensed that someone laid a hand on the baby of the family, the dog took a mouthful of the man's britches and pulled his ample posterior backward. When Rally let go, the man fled up the road and past our house. Our laughter filled the valley.

Chapter 5

Father trudged off to the fields, and Mamma snuck me out to Isaiah's house. Father surely would blow a thunderstorm of cuss words if he found out that we'd set foot on Isaiah's land. My father scorned the man and banned us from going near his home. I knew how to *look the other way* when I passed Isaiah on the road.

Mamma and I stole past Isaiah's towering gate, the only one in our neighborhood. Most neighbors had no gate and left their homes unlocked. I imagined that his house would be larger, matching Isaiah's status as a major landowner in the area. Wooden shutters barred light from entering the rectangular structure. A steep gable roof jutted above pasty walls, making the building gothic, and threatening to the countryside. By the gate, the pinnacle of the cedar trees swayed, but the air inside remained still and clammy.

Isaiah's mute dog fixed its eyes on the distant green hills as if grieving for a loved one. One lazy paw pushed an ear, and he paid us no mind. I wished my dogs, Rally, and Castro, stood by my side. They were superior to this ol' mongrel. They feared nothing, but they stayed home. Did they know Father banned us from crossing into Isaiah's land, or could they sense something sinister under the large cedar trees towering over the massive gate?

Next to the house, Valencia orange trees stood laden with the largest citrus fruits I had ever seen. They were supposed to be the sweetest fruits in the valley, but no local ever tasted Isaiah's forbidden fruits. He threatened to shoot anyone who dared to pick one of his oranges.

Isaiah stumbled on the uneven ground as he ambled toward us. Quickly, he regained his poise and scowled at Mamma and me. He held the bearing of a man in control, but I knew that, like my father, Isaiah was past his prime. Even at six years old, I recognized he wrestled with worries and problems. His long strides could not outpace the haunted look in his hawk eyes.

A small boy my age clutched the man's hand and they lurched toward the graveside. The lad struggled to keep up.

"Sonny, come on." Isaiah jerked the youngster's arm, pressing him to bring his attention to the morbid scene.

"Yes, Daddy sir."

Sonny's eyes wandered off, searching for a way to retreat and cling to the innocence of childhood. His eyes fixed on mine. He might well have been my twin. We had the same green *pus-eyes*, pale skin, and hair tightly coiled like a bucket of black pepper grains.

The pain on his face seemed unbearable. I wanted no kinship with this boy with eyes like my father and his father. I ducked behind Mamma's skirt fearing that his misery might spread to me.

Sonny gripped a small bouquet of white, bell-shaped flowers he'd just plucked from the vine behind their stable. Left on the vine, the flower might remain pure and white for weeks. In Sonny's grasp, they were already wilting in the hot air. He tossed the bouquet with his left hand into the grave. His solitary action struck me as an unfitting tribute to his deceased mother lying at the bottom of the grave beneath the cedar trees.

"Shall we gather at the river," Mamma's warm soprano voice sang out, impervious to the atmosphere of pain. I held on to her waiting for the choking feeling to abate from the air. It persisted like the bad blood between our families.

Father and Isaiah refused to speak to each other because of a dispute that predated my birth. The quarrel started when Father's mother died in 1946. Isaiah came to her house and stole her baking iron.

Father lived in North America when all this happened. He would have stopped Isaiah from setting foot in the family home. Nobody knew if Isaiah still possessed the baking iron, and I began to look for other reasons why Father found him so despicable.

Folks recount how Isaiah shot a prowler who was trying to steal a crocus bag filled with two hundred of his prized Valencia oranges. As the thief lifted the bag to his shoulder, Isaiah blasted him with his shotgun.

My father disagreed with the story. Isaiah's tales always needed clarification.

"Isaiah's blind as a bat," and could shoot nothing. Father explained that Isaiah's night watchman shot the prowler. Isaiah took credit anyway, brandishing his shotgun menacingly as he trotted his horse through the village.

I felt no pity for Sonny, the son of a man who so irked my father. Neither of us understood that sins of the fathers follow their sons. If I felt any pity, it was for the woman lying in the bottom of the freshly dug grave. Still of childbearing age, she suddenly "took sick" and died.

The men at the grave puffed their rum breath into the air. They drank distilled spirits for the dead, and the rum elevated their moods as they shoveled dirt on the woman's coffin.

"Man, that is born from a woman has but a short time to live."

A preacher's solemn voice broke in. The man was a stranger to me. Usually preachers carried grand, leather-bound Bibles, but this parson read from a child's tiny school Bible. He wore a neatly pressed khaki outfit destined for work on the farm. Abandoning his full-time job as a cultivator, he hurried to perform this requiem. Isaiah wanted his woman buried quickly.

Above the leaves of the cedar trees, clouds gathered. A dark cloud in the eastern skies foretold a sudden storm. Hastily, the men shoved the red dirt on to the coffin. Mamma unfurled the red family umbrella as raindrops fell sideways through the cedar trees.

The preacher's voice faded. We hastily exited Isaiah's gloomy world, and the gate creaked shut behind us. One of Sonny's older brothers eyed us as he locked up. They'd shared enough of their private world. Mamma and I climbed up the hill back home. Our dogs, Rally, and Castro glanced up and went back to their doggie dreams.

Soon after the woman's funeral, Isaiah's mystique deepened. A rotting smell clung to the air as gum oozed from age-old fractures on the cedar trees above the grave. The trees were not dying, however. Every year they grew larger, and the large, green lizards that took up residence on the branches got bigger and bolder.

When anyone approached, the green lizards defiantly pumped up on all fours until their color turned blacker than the shadows at the bottom of our deepest valley. The lizards glared with blood-red eyes, daring anyone to come closer. This transformation entrenched local belief that these lizards were ghosts.

Isaiah sent Sonny to live with relatives in the big city. The lizards became part of the landscape that shrouded the mystery of the woman's death. That suited Isaiah's sinister guise. He barred people from peeking around his property. I clamped my mouth shut and hustled past the cedar trees whenever I walked that road.

Chapter 6

My brother, Serge, and I forgot about our day in school and climbed the hillside behind our home. Below, the narrow valley extending past Isaiah's land fell motionless in the afternoon light. All day long the sun spent its energy lifting moisture into the clear blue sky. No breeze moved the fruit trees decking the hillside. The *thud-thud* of men hoeing the soil ceased.

After a day of digging mounds to plant his yams, Father lumbered homeward up the hill. Sweat mixed with dried dirt formed a stiff cast around his waist. He thrusted his machete in the crack between two planks on the kitchen wall and then tumbled into his favorite perch under the mango tree.

Above the valley, a chicken hawk on the hunt soared on the updraft eyeing everything below. The hawk's high-pitched call signaled that it spotted a litter of Mamma's chickens foraging in the yard. The piercing cry scattered the litter and exposed the chicks that were too slow to reach the cover of the mother wings. A slow chick might become dinner for a hawk.

Rally and Castro heard the chicken hawk's hunting call and charged to save the chicks. The dogs circled the brood and shot their fiercest bark at the soaring predator. The hawk flapped away, seeking easier prey.

Gradually, the afternoon sun lost its hold on the valley and retreated to leave a sculpture of shadows at the foot of the western slopes. Serge and I climbed higher. The sun still glowed on the slopes. It shone through the scrub bushes and polished the rod-wood berries to an inky sheen. We went after the sweet, juicy berries on the rod-wood bushes.

From next door, Wesley and his brother joined us. Wesley had just grown his first two permanent front teeth. They stood large and strong with a welcome depicting his zest for life.

"Tucky axe," we teased him because his teeth were too large for his mouth.

He smiled his new teeth as he kept an eye on his younger brother, a tumbling toddler. The younger sibling barely smiled and spoke only tentatively. The boys and a teenage brother, Dieldrin, lived with their aging grandparents in the house beside us.

The brothers were waiting for their mother "to send for them" to live with her in New York City. The "Immigration" was delaying her green card application. While he lingered, Wesley boasted that he would soon leave for a better life in New York.

Serge romped in the midst of the action, practicing his cynical humor and testing the limits of his pranks. Adults left us to our play. As the oldest of the boys, I helped set boundaries in the pack, making sure they stayed away from the poison berries. In innocence, we clung to the changing light of the afternoon, heedless of the fact that both soon would end.

Our laughter filled the hillside. We bent the branches on the rod-wood trees, picked the berries, and sucked the juice. In delight, we flicked the seeds off the tip of our tongues and watched them disappear in the bushes. Every grinning face displayed the inky stain from the berries.

Below, a blue "young smoke" drifted lazily above the corrugated zinc roof of our outdoor kitchen. Young smoke meant Mamma had just started a blazing fire to cook dinner. No aroma effused from the kitchen. Nothing was ready yet. We played on.

When the yam and breadfruit cooked, Mamma "drew" the wood and lowered the flame. Young smoke died. The smell of onions and herbs simmering in hot oil drifted up to where we played. I smelled pork strips sizzling in the frying pan. I could almost taste the dumplings she always served with fried pork.

"Time to draw near."

Mamma adopted the line from a popular church hymn to call us to dinner. We abandoned our neighbors and hustled home. Dinnertime was a private occasion in our family. People left us alone to eat a meal ample in starch and lean in protein.

My father sat silent at the head of the table. He ate heartily. A hefty meal fueled his energy for hard work on the farm the next day. Just as Mamma served dinner, Mass Harry broke the rule and interrupted dinner with a visit. *Mass* was a shortening of the term *master* from our colonial heritage. Nobody used Mister in everyday talk.

Father ignored him. Mamma offered him dinner.

"No," he responded. "Me no eat pork."

Mamma knew Mass Harry, the deacon at the local church, believed pigs were unclean and unfit for eating. Father, too, never ate pork. Pork grease gave him indigestion, and there was nothing fouler than his mood when he had an upset stomach.

Father despised dumplings. He only dined on what produce grew on our farm. Mamma, quick to comply with his needs, always made him a meal of codfish stew and yams. However, Father ate all his codfish. The little bit of fish could only feed one man.

Mass Harry walked up to one of the huge cedar trees behind our outhouse and fixed his gaze high up on the branches. I thought he might be counting the innumerable seedpods on the tree.

"Hum, it is ripe." His Adam's apple moved as he spoke.

Still staring upward, one hand clasped his church-hat to his head lest it fall irreverently to the earth. A reddish undertone flushed his dark skin and highlighted his handsome face. Mass Harry, a sawyer-man, had the skill to chop down our cedar trees without mashing down the outhouse or the citrus trees nearby.

He continued to poke his chin at the tree, and his voice came out with an unusual reverence, seemingly from a higher place. His Adam's apple bumped up and down again.

"Aahye," he mumbled with finality. This was a contraction of "ah yes," with a softer sound and a gentle accord among friends.

"Tomorrow," he promised as he finished surveying where he would drop the tree. He left on the long walk to his home in Thatch Walk.

Chapter 7

The next day, I came home for lunch to find no meal waiting. I threw a tantrum.

"A want muh lunch," I complained.

I sat on the retaining rock wall next to the kitchen and bawled. My cousin Gene watched my tantrum with detachment. He ate with us because he lived too far way to go home for lunch and get back to school in time.

Amid my outburst, I saw Mamma's brown legs behind the kitchen door. She was playing her usual hide and seek with me. Smiling, she showed me the lunch she hid under a towel. I tried to swallow the feeling that I shouldn't have doubted her in the first place.

Though a prankster, Gene quickly tailored his mischief while in our house. At an earlier time, Rally came to watch Gene and me wrestling, trying to throw each other to the ground. Rally may have sensed that the older Gene might hurt me because he slipped behind and bit Gene's leg.

Gene changed the weather when he cried. His mouth opened to show rows of irregular teeth that made him look broken and sad. I knew him all my life, but he wailed as if I'd set my killer dog on him. I dropped my eyes to the ground and shared my cousin's sadness.

Mamma tenderly patched him up, talking softly to him as she bandaged his leg. She called him "Pa Gene" after his father "Pa Sam," an unflappable man. Gene calmed down. Mamma had a way with wounds and wounded spirits.

After lunch, we went to see what caused the rasping sound behind our house. Mass Harry perched on a platform pumping a long saw through a cedar log. His son worked with him. While we were at school, they cut the cedar tree, skillfully dropping it between the outhouse and the citrus trees.

"That's a sawpit." Gene pointed at the platform.

The men built the sawpit slightly taller than a man. They secured the top of the ramp to a sturdy breadfruit tree while the lower end trailed to the ground. The men cut the cedar tree into logs and then rolled a piece to the top of the ramp. They were sawing the log to make flat boards.

Mass Harry poised on top of the structure and pushed the saw through the log. His son remained on the ground pulling the other end of the long, two-handled-saw. The youngster pulled when his father pushed, and the saw's teeth ripped through the log, rasping out their coordination. The air hushed each time the blade bit into the wood. They worked as if we were invisible. We watched quietly, shadows in an adult world.

"Me want to go at kid head," the youngster muttered. Mass Harry gave his monosyllabic confirmation. They stopped sawing and switched positions on the sawpit. New to the trade, his son got tired easily. He wanted to work the saw from the top of the log. From above, he pushed down while his dad performed the harder job of pulling.

"Me want to go at kid foot," he requested when he got tired of working the top. Sawdust fell sideways ahead of the blade, and we itched to play in its soft flakes. Mamma sent us back to the little schoolhouse next door, where the termites tunneled through the woodwork and built nests in the ceiling.

We came home from school and watched as the men packed up for the day. They left a neat pile of sawdust under the sawpit. The men fitted a slotted piece of bamboo over the jagged teeth of the saw. Mass Harry hoisted it to his shoulder. He set out for the three-mile walk home to Thatch Walk.

After another day of sawing, they reduced the cedar tree to a stack of neatly cut planks. They cut each plank slightly longer than a tall man. The boards were a stretch of flawless cinnamon red hue. It held the same warm appeal as the rich soil that nourished our crops.

The men leaned the planks against the breadfruit tree and left them to cure in the shade. When the wood dried, my sisters and I helped Father carry the lumber to the cellar. In the cured form, the smell of death that haunted Isaiah's cedar trees vanished from the wood.

Folks prized cedarwood for building or making furniture, but my father kept secret the reason he guarded these boards so carefully. He tucked them away in two waist high piles in the dark cellar beneath our house.

Chapter 8

My brother and I played with our neighbor Wesley, but would never dare play with Dieldrin, their older brother. Dieldrin earned the label *enemy number one* for the trouble he caused my family. He made up limericks using Father's punchy lines to torment us, but he never teased my tough father to his face. Instead, he tormented my sister Hazel.

Even as we played, Hazel was suffering Dieldrin's taunts as she walked home from school. He made fun of her light complexion, her green "puss eyes," and the mop of curly, red hair ablaze on her head.

My sister showed all the supposed contradictions of our mixed ancestry. She inherited the pale skin from my mother's Welsh side of the family, the light eyes from my father's European lineage, and the dense curls inherited from African blood on both sides of the family tree. Not one person had her shock of red hair. People in our district often reminded her that she was an oddity.

Hazel's face turned red in shame as she told us Dieldrin called her red as a *dun dus,* an albino. Even though she was not an albino, she got hell for coming closer than most. For what seemed like years, we listened to Hazel's complaints. Father spat in disgust at the ground and fumed.

Not even our property escaped Dieldrin's wrath. The boy ripped the heart out the June plum fruit tree behind our kitchen. He even shot out our dog's eye with his slingshot.

Nobody knew his father, and his mother left him in the care of his aging grandparents next door. Tearfully, Mamma pleaded with his folks, and they ignored her. His ailing grandfather, once a prominent citizen, was unable to chase a teenage boy. The man, faltering in the grip of "ol' age," stared blankly into space. The grandmother tried to explain the aging man's condition.

"Ol' age sickness ketch up with him."

Any day now, the bells at Refuge, the Anglican Church with the big cemetery, may clang out his passing.

Secretly, I despised Dieldrin as much as he scorned my family, but I hid my feelings. I dreaded the angry scowl that hung off his face. Hoping to ease the worries and problems between the families, I tried to befriend him.

"Patchy, patchy trousiz," he responded, laughing at my makeshift trousers that the tailor stitched from remnants of two different shades of khaki cloth. His caustic laugh, intended to torment, failed to light his bloodshot eyes. Though I liked the pants, I refused to wear them again. I preferred to hide my shame rather than face Dieldrin's scorn.

One Friday afternoon, Father and I were returning home after he picked breadfruits from our field next to Isaiah's house. I strained up the hill lugging two of the huge fruits in each hand. Father carried the long pole that he used to pick the breadfruits off the tree. We came around a bend and ran face to face with Dieldrin and three of his companions meandering home from school. Father pretended that he hadn't seen them. They edged closer.

Suddenly, Father twitched his shoulder and sent the pole flying. The long pole fell to the ground, bounced a few times, and fell silent. Dieldrin and his friends broke into little scared packs. Father grabbed a rock the size of my head and hurled it at Dieldrin. The rock skipped near his feet, following his path, but it never hit him. Dieldrin ran for his life along a rock wall that marked the boundary between our properties. The other boys retreated up the hill toward the school.

Angry screams blazed from next door as Dieldrin took the back-way home and informed his grandparents that my father almost killed him with rock-stones. The grandmother cursed my father with more sins than I knew he had.

I sat with my father under the mango, wordlessly siding with him as he spat in disgust on the ground. I hoped he might tell the ol' woman to "shut her rass up," but he kept his lips tightly sealed. Late into the evening as the shadows dropped into the bottom below our house, she got tired and quieted. Father had made his point though, and Dieldrin stopped pestering my family.

Chapter 9

Before Christmas, Mass Harry's senile mother wandered away from her home and jumped into the damp bosom of a sinkhole. Nobody wanted the task of going all the way to Thatch Walk to retrieve her corpse from that hole.

Father took his block and tackle from the toolbox and greased the pulleys, muttering he would show them how to bring the body up from the sinkhole. I wondered why he would go to faraway Thatch Walk for such a morbid quest. Thankfully, he left me home.

He returned well past dinnertime. Tired but full of accomplishment, he described how he used the pulleys to lower a man on a piece of cedar board into the hole. The man rolled the corpse onto the board. Father then used the pulley to hoist the woman's remains to the surface.

Father refused to eat dinner. He offered no explanation, and nobody prodded him. We knew from his puffed upper lip that we should leave him alone.

Since the dead woman was the mother of the godly deacon, I thought folks should not fear her ghost. They explained that only a troubled soul committed suicide, and they saw her ghost like every other village dead.

At school, one of the boys from Thatch Walk talked about ghosts. He confided that he was born with a *caul*, an extra flap of skin over his eyes. A caul gave him the unique power to see ghosts. We leaned closer, watching his eyes widen. His voice grew hoarse with emotion.

"Not everyone can see a *duppy*."

A *duppy* is a ghost returning to haunt its old territory.

"Ah see the ol' woman's duppy at the sinkhole."

"How you know is her?" Mass Harry's youngest daughter asked suspiciously.

"From the corner of muh eye, a see her red *tie-head*."

We knew the woman always wore a red bandana on her head. The boy whispered that the old woman vanished when he turned to look at her. He became tongue-tied, and his scream caught in his throat. The *duppy* made his head swell up. He showed us how he turned his shirt inside out to ward off the spirit or else would have frothed at the mouth and fainted.

I curled my bare feet in the red dirt and wiped my sweaty hands on my pants. The *duppy* season peaked at Christmas time. Most people went to bed at dusk to avoid running into the woman's ghost in the dark. Only brave young men took to the roads to visit their sweethearts in the next village.

Just before bedtime, Father declared that we were leaving on a trip to the market in Mountain. He wanted to buy beef for Christmas dinner. He planned to leave before daybreak, the most haunted part of the night. In the dark, we would pass by the sinkhole haunted by the woman's ghost. Visions of the ghostly bandana kept me up all night.

Father could buy meat from the local butcher at the crossroad; instead, he dragged me on a five-mile ordeal up to Mountain. *Why did he sell the donkey that took me across the hills to see the "Chiney" doctor?*

He claimed that the animal bolted out of control with him on the packsaddle. He faked anger at the donkey, trying to mask his inability to control a normally docile animal. I found it hard to believe that our donkey suddenly turned bad, nor would I accept that my aging father was losing control of the farm animals.

Chapter 10

Father woke me up in the dark, long before the dawn of "red clouds" cut the grip of the night on the land. Reluctantly, I dressed in the soft glow of the kerosene lamp. I hated getting up in the dark.

Coffee dripped from the cotton bag in the outdoor kitchen. He handed me a half-filled mug. Strong as ever, it bit into my stomach as I swallowed. Warmth rushed over my body and a few sips were more than enough. I tossed the rest into the black of the night and slipped on my cap.

Tentatively, I treaded into the dark as the weak, amber beam from the flashlight pointed the way. The moon, that earlier flooded our valley with light, had slipped away, ducking past the hills behind Isaiah's house. A faint glow outlined the peaks, but no gleam penetrated our valley. The same rotting smell from the cedar trees filled the air as I tiptoed past Isaiah's gate.

Daylight "soon come," yet darkness clutched the land as if it were midnight. Even the dogs slept at this ungodly hour that folks called "young night." No other father got up this early on the morn before Christmas Eve nudging his son along paths that few knew existed.

From time to time, Father paused to catch his breath. He complained of "shortness," fretting how he couldn't move as fast as he used to. Despite his waning vigor, Father's reputation for high energy still stuck. As he rested, I stood with the patience of our companion dog, Rally. His inner strength soon surged back to fire his muscles. I heard his call in the dark.

"Come." And we moved on.

Father found his way effortlessly through the predawn monochromatic landscape. He trained me how to walk in the dark. He shone the light at my feet as I plodded ahead of him and turned as he pointed the flashlight at each bend.

Our ascent to Mountain took us right past the sinkhole where Mass Harry's mother killed herself. The red bandana appeared in my head. My heart thundered, but I kept my worries tight to my chest. In Father's company, you show no weakness.

The air smelled like rotting wood as we approached the sinkhole. Except for the tiny beam of our flashlight, everything remained black. Nearby, a jackass stamped impatiently and snorted in irritation. Something disturbed the peace. The hills echoed the single howl of a dog, and then a deathlike silence filled the gorge. The flashlight flickered. We paused.

"Wait." Father's voice rasped.

He handed the flashlight to me as his hand reached in his pocket. One of his Giants, a red fire-cracker emerged. He struck a match and the orange flame flickered in a breeze that sprang out of nowhere. He used me as a shield and tried to light the fuse. In the fickle light, the shadow of his hat danced on the rocks behind him.

Suddenly the fuse flared. Father tossed the Giant across the gulley. We waited for the thunder. The blast ruptured the stillness of the night air and sent echoes bouncing from hill to hill.

In the quiet afterwards, I heard the echoes of frantic footsteps breaking away from the terror of the explosion. My father offered a simple explanation for this predawn bombardment.

"Clear de way."

The darkness hid my smile. My father would get me through this dark night. We moved on.

The flashlight lit up ghostly figures on the foliage ahead of our path. I lost my faith. Every bush held a duppy. My head grew to the size of a watermelon, and I got tongue-tied and could not find my voice to scream. The hair on the back of my neck prickled as a cold shiver ran down my back.

I heard my father's regular breathing behind me. He showed no sign of fear. Maybe he was not born with a caul over his eyes and he couldn't see the duppy that I saw. He would surely cuss me if I stopped and turned my shirt inside out to ward off the spirits. I stumbled on, listening to my pounding heart.

What appeared as a duppy thirty feet away, materialized as a clump of the common "bitter bush," its silver Christmas flowering reflecting the dim light. I felt embarrassed that my fear of an ordinary bush made my head swell up. The melon that was my head shrunk back to fit under my cap.

Chapter 11

Dawn came unwillingly, hesitating to challenge the power of the night. Forms took shape in a quixotic landscape of huge, leafless guangu trees waving limbs bearded with wild-pine air plants. Responding to a shorter day length, the trees had shed all their leaves. Now they were keeping a keen eye for the gentle rains that heralded spring.

We walked silently among the lofty plants. Usually diversity is the hallmark of the tropics, and deciduous trees are randomly scattered. Someone long ago must have planted these guangu trees as shade for a coffee plantation or a cattle farm.

The trees bade us farewell in sad voices born from the light breeze rushing through their branches. The branches rubbed against each other and groaned. Moisture formed on my clothes and gave teeth to the wind. The grass underfoot felt soggy with dew. This was my favorite time to sleep and Father's favorite time to meet the day.

I plodded on, looking for the morn. At the end of the pasture, he pulled two strands of barbed wire apart for me to slip through. In turn, I did the same for him. In the quiet period before sunrise, we left the narrow path for the dark asphalt road leading up to the market in Mountain.

Daybreak came with a haste to forget the night. Dew on the huge leaves of the breadfruit trees caught sunlight and lit up with life. Spider webs shimmered as moisture on the webbing glowed.

Folks who worked their trade during the week came to the market to sell their wares on the weekend. The fresh smell of wicker baskets filled the air as we strolled down neat rows of merchandise. Brightly colored *bankras,* baskets weaved from indigenous palm leaves, decorated the stalls. My father moved among these strangers with ease. They shared some common fraternity that boys didn't understand.

We stopped to buy meat from a man whose skin denied the power of the tropical sun. His skin flowed flawlessly as midnight on a starless night, and his eyes glowed with the warmth of live coals on a bulletwood fire. Father placed his order.

"Five pound a shoulder round." He could buy more beef, but meat spoils quickly in the heat. Nobody except the shopkeeper at the crossroad owned a refrigerator.

The butcher's handsaw ripped through meat and bone. He wrapped the cut in brown paper, and Father placed it in a double-lined plastic bag that Mamma had made on her sewing machine. That would keep the meat fresh until we got home.

Before we left the market, we bought some *head sugar* from a woman displaying them in a huge bamboo basket. Folks made head sugar by boiling sugarcane juice to a crystalized lump. The lump felt harder than my head, so Father took out his black-handled pocketknife and hacked off a piece. I munched, savoring the stimulating taste of ginger. He bought nothing for himself, but he got Mamma a new grater to shred sweet potatoes for her puddings.

Our neighbors were still asleep when we slipped back in the valley. Only my family got up early for Christmas. Father confessed that, decades earlier, he took this same walk with his father, Ol' Joe. During the night, I almost died of fright a thousand times, and I lumbered past superstitions dear to people in the village. If there were ghosts, I should have seen them as I stumbled along the haunted path from young night to dawn. The walk forever erased my fear of ghosts.

Chapter 12

Mid-morning and the valley below our home is still thick with the mist of evaporating dew. It is spring again, and the Spanish Needle flowers flood the air with a sugary aroma. My sister Jan and I strolled through the valley, up the stony road beyond our home, and edged into the level where Salaman and his family lived. We paused next to our family's disputed land by the roadside. Father's older brother, Uncle Mack, owned the land, but he'd left home to work the sugarcane fields in Cuba. Uncle Buster, another brother, assumed control of the property and made Salaman overseer of the fields.

As the village lawyer, Salaman advised people on land deals and wrote wills without charging a penny. He regularly read the newspaper and kept up with events in the world. If you crossed him, he may well set his hateful wife to curse you out the district. You could not guess Salaman orchestrated it all from behind his newspaper. He smiled in your face.

Uncle Buster, too, charmed folks and got Salaman to do his every bidding. He mastered the art of disarming people with his big smile and his loud greetings. A blunt man, Father warmed up to you if you worked hard and talked politics. He only spoke to people whom he liked.

To maintain his integrity as a leading citizen, Salaman didn't appear in public with his venomous wife. Still, he fathered more than a dozen children with her. Any child from their long list of offspring, could slander a neighbor from sunup to sundown.

His wife and her children took their verbal abuse to the streets and attacked without shame. Nighttime did not stop them. From their house, next to the giant cottonwood tree, they ran from shop to shop degrading whomever they saw fit. The giant tree stood for over a hundred years, and its branches spread to overshadow the homes in the valley.

The mother, the most venomous of the pack, led their nightly stampede. Nobody could contend with her tongue. Anyone who respected their mother would never repeat her words.

To avoid their scorn, most people made peace with the family. My father differed from most people. He openly challenged the wild ways of the women, and they frustrated him with their bitter taunts. With his family of wrath, Salaman barred father from having access to his brother's land, the most fertile land in our area.

Rooster, Salaman's teenage son, joined the pack of women eying my sister and me as we paused by Uncle Mack's land. When he was a preteen, Rooster had fallen out of an ackee tree. Fortunately, a branch broke his descent before he crashed to the unyielding ground thirty feet below. The branch that saved him fractured one of the bones in his face. After he healed, one of his eyes wandered off, gazing at some unseen object. Local idiom called this lack of ocular focus, "look a bush."

Normally, if you were different, people made fun of you, but not a soul dared to make fun of Rooster's eye. If you dared, you had to confront his family, and this would open a blood feud lasting three generations.

Reading and arithmetic eluded Rooster, and he dropped out of school.

"He don't know 'A' from bull foot," Salaman grumbled about his illiterate son.

Rooster made up for his lack of learning with his machete. I saw him split a coconut, larger than a man's head, with a mere flick of his blade.

The youngster wore his shirt open to show his muscular chest as well as powerful forearms. He had long outgrown his bell-bottomed pants, and they flared above his ankles. He planted his bare feet on the dirt with heels touching and toes spread outward in a sharp V-shape. In that stance, he appeared as if he might topple over when he stepped forward. He walked fine, however.

Rooster fixed his good eye on me. The other wandered. I followed the wandering eye. True to legend, the eye looked to the bushes. Unsure which eye to make contact with, I looked at his feet and hoped to escape his wrath.

"Leave this place alone, man. It is no good a rass."

Rooster's voice interrupted my thoughts as he mocked my father. He was brilliant. He copied Father's intonation, volume, and speech patterns remarkably well for an illiterate young man. His mouth opened to show perfectly formed teeth as he heckled and laughed. Why should a young man so down on his luck make fun of my father and me?

True, Father often advocated that life in these hills was "no good." Families followed the same paths as their ancestors, living in poverty or working themselves into the ground trying to avoid that outcome. Anyone with a few dollars earned it away from the hills. Rooster might be better off if he left "this place" of his birth, but he saw no value in the saying attributed to Father.

"Dan-Dan, ol' pan, Dan-Dan, man," Rooster heckled as he copied Father's speech pattern to make a jingle out of my name. My skin prickled. He sounded just like Father, but it was all nonsense. Father never once repeated my name as I always jumped the first time he called for me. He despised slackers.

Folks attributed many sayings to my father. Few were true. Rooster's imitation of my father bothered me. Anyone listening must think I was the son of the village idiot. Should I be ashamed of a quirky father who walked too fast, and worked too hard to feed his family?

Rooster followed me around, delighting his relatives with his teasing. Salaman, his father, glanced over his newspaper, gave a signal, and urged him on. As I walked away, Rooster lost his smile, and his eye went back to looking at the boring bushes. It would not be the last time I heard someone make fun of my father.

At dusk, my father washed up my brother and me for bed. Later, I sat with Serge and our two sisters at the dining room table, staring at the worn pages of the old storybook. We read whatever words we knew and made up stories about the pictures of Grendel's long nails clawing across the pages. The kerosene lamp cast tall shadows of our heads on the walls and kept at bay the ghosts of our grandparents who once lived in our ol' house.

Early to bed as always, Father's voice called out. "Dan-Dan, bring me a mug a water." At once, I filled the white enamel mug and carried it to him.

Mamma's workday lasted long into the night. Her voice came in song from the outdoor kitchen. She loved to sing.

From the shadows on the road below our house, Rooster's mom yelled out in rebuke. She made stinging remarks about my father. We fell silent and listened. For a woman incapable of deciphering *"A" from bull foot*, she sure knew how to hurt with words.

"Fart stink. You fart stink," she teased.

I wondered why Father failed to stand up to that woman. Sometimes I heard him whispering an animated soliloquy as if quarrelling with the devil-woman. When he won the battle, he became calm, but he never confronted her. There was not enough time left on Earth to win a clash with the woman and her family. In the silence, I failed to see the side of my father that many people in my community sought to deride.

The kerosene lamp struggled to keep the darkness away. Forms carved into the bulletwood mantelpiece above the door grew a tail as menacing as the black scorpion's stinger. A moth drawn to the flames found its way into the lamp. It fluttered and filled the lampshade with the dust of its wings before it perished. Next day, when the lamp cooled, I puffed the dust of the moth to the winds.

Chapter 13

Around the corner from Salaman's giant silk cottonwood tree, Cousin Pa Sam lived with his family. One of the tallest men in our neighborhood, Pa Sam's head rose above the bushes when he sat on his chestnut horse. Named Samuelson at birth, his many children changed his name to the easier-sounding contraction.

When my siblings and I ran into Pa Sam, we hollered "Mawning, Pa Sam." He bellowed a cheerful response.

"A howdy mi picinniny?" His deep voice bounced back from the hills. We replied just as lively.

"Mi hearty."

His voice bore a slight Scottish accent, common to the older folks in our village. Some of the elder people traced their ancestry to the colonial days when Scottish and Irish overseers ran the plantations for their English overlords. After the decline of the colonial system, descendants of the overseers retreated to live on the fruitful slopes of the mountains. They blended their genes with descendants of African slaves and learned to coexist. Like my family, Pa Sam was a mixture of both worlds. His light skin marked his European ancestry, and his tightly curled hair marked his African roots.

On weekends, when I came home from elementary school, my dad often took me to visit Pa Sam. The fragrant Sweet Margaret plants welcomed us as we approached the meadow where Pa Sam pastured his horse. Gene, my best friend since preschool, called out for me to join him on one of his pranks.

We left our fathers sitting by the kitchen sipping coffee while Gene showed me how to make a slingshot. He whipped out his pocketknife and whittled a Y-shaped stick to form the handle. Patiently, he cut a strip from an old shoe and made the pouch. When he finished making the gadget, he taught me how to shoot.

We walked through the citrus groves looking for birds to shoot. Dim light filtered through trees to the ground and made a habitat for the white-belly dove, the biggest and most elusive bird in the wild. Gene pointed out the traps he set to catch the prized birds.

He made the traps by weaving saplings to form a small basket. He then inverted the basket and camouflaged it with dried leaves. He fixed a string loop to act as a trigger. If the dove landed on the loop to feed, the basket fell, trapping the bird.

We avoided the coffee grove sheltered by the huge silk-cotton tree. Here the canopy blocked light from filtering to the ground. Mosquitoes swarmed in droves haunting the twilight conditions. Nobody entered those groves unless they ignited a small *green bush* fire to fumigate the area with smoke.

As we hiked, Gene described the fire lantern bird with fanciful feathers and a plump chest. The bird, he explained, had a mottled brown body and a fire-red breast. I tested my slingshot and waited for a chance to fire into its fleshy torso.

We saw no birds to shoot. They avoided the heat of the day, preferring to feed in the cool of the morning or the waning light of the evening. We did not know any better, but I would follow Gene anywhere in search of birds with fanciful feathers.

We returned to his house and watched his older brother make sugar cane juice. His brother chopped stems of sugar cane from the plot behind the fowl coop. He shaved off the leaves and washed the sugar cane press.

Long ago, Pa Sam had constructed the press by planting a wooden post in the ground. He carved a waist-high opening through the post. Gene pressed a lever through the opening while I fed pieces of sugar cane under the lever. I listened to the *crack-crack* as he crushed the sugar cane. Juice swooshed down into a bucket. Gene handed me a white enamel mug filled with the cool, refreshing liquid.

We were forbidden from playing around the tank that held Pa Sam's drinking water. Gene led me to explore it anyway. We climbed onto the cement wall, and he pulled back one of the corrugated zinc panels covering the tank. He pointed to the horrors that lay waiting for me if I fell in. His voice hushed as we gaped into the shimmering water.

"Raw head and bloody bone. Suck you blood."

Gene tried to point out the blood red of the creature swimming among the ripples. Light slipped into the tank from a crack in the roof and created phantom figures in the ripples. I almost glimpsed the monsters waiting below, and with a little imagination, coaxed on by Gene, I smelled their bloody bones.

Chapter 14

Pa Sam married Antoinette, a woman of Asian extraction. Her children called her Ma Ann, and everyone followed suit. While he towered, she barely rose to his waist. Years of smoking a short, stubby pipe left her with a voice almost as deep as his. Ma Ann's voice held the warmest ring, particularly for my younger brother Serge, whom she jokingly called her boyfriend.

On Fridays, she pulled her son Gene out of school to help her collect produce for the market in town. Sometimes Ma Ann visited our house to gather fruits for market. She always wore a red bandana on her head. Her hair, rumored to extend past her buttocks, never saw daylight.

On one of her visits, Mamma offered to sell Ma Ann some green-skinned pumpkins still growing on the vine. Mamma could not determine if these pumpkins were ready for harvesting because they stayed the same color even when mature. Ma Ann took up the challenge. She groped in her apron and whipped out a small pocketknife. The smell of tobacco drifted into the air. She often carried a twist of homegrown tobacco to smoke in her short, stubby pipe.

Ma Ann slipped the blade into one of the pumpkins and cut out a small triangle. She lifted it to show Mamma. Light caught the pale golden hue from the belly of the pumpkin.

"See it there. They need time to get ready," Ma Ann proclaimed in her authoritative voice.

The flesh of a mature pumpkin should be a brighter orange color. She slipped the triangle back in the fruit. Sap oozed around the cut as the pumpkin accepted the reinsertion without harm. The crop continued to grow until she came back weeks later and took the pumpkins to the market.

My father always seemed relaxed when we visited Pa Sam. On one of our Saturday visits, Father borrowed Salaman's newspaper and shared an article with Pa Sam. Ma Ann stood by the fire turning a ladle in a big, black cauldron. Her plaid bandana wrapped tightly around her hair. Despite the firm line on her lips, her eyes burned with contentment. She often cooked for her dozen children.

Father read the headlines and pointed to a picture of people fleeing from Cuba to escape their new ruler. Pa Sam looked away from the paper. Events in the rest of the outside world mattered little to him.

"Mi eyes dark, can't see."

He opted out of admitting he could not read *"A" from bull foot.*

Father fretted about his brother, Mack Martin, who'd left home fifty years ago. Mack was trying to escape Cuba. Suddenly, Father doubled over and sobbed, spilling tears to the ground. Everyone hushed and stared at the tough man who cried so tenderly. For the first time, I saw a grown man cry.

I played with Gene a little longer than usual, using this detachment to insulate me from my father's angst. Not a soul offered any words of comfort. Ma Ann stopped turning the ladle in mid-stroke and reached for her short, stubby pipe. Pa Sam sat unmoved, very little moved him.

Gene and I dropped our eyes to our feet and shared a little of Father's grief in silence. In our pastoral existence, words of empathy were as scarce as water during the long, dry season on our limestone soil.

Father soon composed himself. He kicked his boots at the traces of moisture where his tears landed on the ground. The wet spots quickly dried in the heat, erasing the evidence of his ungluing. Ma Ann puffed her pipe, and silently resumed stirring her cornmeal porridge.

When we left Pa Sam's house, my father seemed calm and resolved. I trotted along with him wondering about his brother who left for the cane fields of Cuba.

Back at home, I followed Gene's lead and climbed the wall of our drinking water tank to see if "raw head and bloody bones" prowled beneath the zinc roof. Light filtered through a crack in the roof and made the same shimmering forms as Gene's tank. Raw head and bloody bones eluded me, however, but Gene's tales kept me from getting close enough to tumble in. A week earlier, one of my classmates had drowned in his family's tank and ruined their valuable drinking water.

Chapter 15

Uncle Mack showed up at our house one afternoon with a straw hat perched elegantly on his head. Father jumped up when he saw Uncle emerge from the car and led us in a hasty procession to meet his brother at the foot of the hill.

Uncle swung his leather suitcase from the car with ease and walked up the hill to our house. Though older than Father, he displayed the same energy that belied their age.

My father pranced from foot to foot, hunting for the words to welcome his brother who'd left home fifty years earlier. Uncle Mack took it all in stride, spreading his smile to wash over us and opening a door to everyone's heart.

My other uncle, Buster, dropped Mack off at our house. Buster owned the only car for hire in the neighborhood. No love existed between Buster and the other brothers. While Uncle Mack toiled away in the sugarcane fields in Cuba, Buster seized control of his land. Without Uncle Mack's permission, Buster sold off some acres of his land and pocketed the money.

My father remained bitter about the shady land dealings, and he avoided Buster, sometimes hiding behind a bush when his brother's car approached. Uncle Mack's arrival from Cuba suddenly shifted the control of the remainder of land out of Buster's hand. The car drove off unceremoniously with Buster's grim face staring ahead.

Father had sent some money to Cuba to help secure Uncle Mack's return. Uncle brought no gifts in the large suitcase that he opened to show us. He told Mamma that he left home in Camagüey with a suitcase of clothes, but at every checkpoint, the authorities took an item. They left him with a few garments. He showed little regret, however. He seemed happy to be home since he'd grown up under the roof of this ol' house that we now lived in. Mamma extended her warm smile to him, and he fit right into our lives.

Everything stopped when Uncle's happy laugh rang out. His easygoing manner and charm with women drew people to him. He reclaimed his land from Uncle Buster and began to install a barbed wire fence around the property.

Uncle Mack left at dawn, and when I came home from elementary school, he had not returned. He had just turned seventy years, and I wondered how he fared at hard labor.

Just before nightfall, he stumbled home. His hands were bloody, and he remained unusually quiet. A satisfied look played at the corner of his lips. I couldn't imagine how an old man ran a fence around several acres of land in one day.

Mamma dressed his hands carefully, using one of the many clean, white bandages that she kept in the top drawer of the antique dresser. Both my parents were excellent at treating wounds. We lived twenty miles away from the nearest doctor in town, and a donkey could only carry him a few miles.

Father often told the story of how he fixed his nephew Victor's fractured arm. One of Father's goats broke Victor's arm as he tried to restrain it. My dad used a homemade splint to set the arm and then brought the boy to get medical attention. The doctor took one look at the splint, checked the bandage, and complimented my father on a job "well done." The doctor sent Victor back home to recover in my father's care.

Mamma's skill with home remedy came with the title of Dr. Gentles, the doctor with the gentle touch. I saw her perform surgery on a hen that fell ill with an overstuffed crop. Mamma cut open the hen's crop, relieved it of its contents, and sewed it back up. The bird walked away from the surgery and became one of her best layers.

Uncle Mack responded well to Mamma's treatments, and by weekend the bandages were off. On Saturday, I followed Father to fetch dried wood to cook our meals. As we passed Uncle Mack's property, I checked to see if his fence held up to my father's standard of work. Bold wooden fence posts supported tightly strung barbed wires. Uncle Mack lived up to the family tradition for hard work.

The brothers had little else in common. The *thud-thud* echoes of my father's hoe on the hard soil always filled our valley. His machete rang out ceaselessly as he slashed the bamboo poles he used to support the yam vines. Uncle knew how to *tek* it easy and he helped our family learn to relax.

He made up a name for people, places, or things. We assumed that he might have forgotten the English words after spending more than fifty years in Cuba. Other times we excused his oversight as the ways of an ol' man.

He called the revered toilet the "shit house," ignoring its proper name. His vulgarity did not offend me. He had a way of softening the edges off the jagged parts of life.

Uncle became a safety valve for the tension between my father and mother. My parents were inherently different. Father saw life as an anxious, hard-driving struggle to work and support his family. Mamma patiently sought her way through the same struggle. When Father lost his temper with Mamma, Uncle Mack reprimanded him gently.

"Take it easy Bro Sal."

Uncle used Mamma's favorite name for Father but mispronounced it and added a touch of levity to our flawed family circle.

Father landed some hefty rebuke on Uncle for meddling in his quarrel. He reminded Mack that he "bought him out of Cuba for ten English pounds." Uncle stayed quiet. I was shocked to hear father turn on the same brother for whom he'd cried so shamelessly at Pa Sam's house.

Mamma retreated away from the conflict to feed the chicken before dusk. The discord wiped the pretty smile off her face, and her eyes lost some of their twinkle. By nightfall, Mamma had composed herself. She loved to sing. We often fell asleep to her songs from the hymnbook.

> A sunbeam, a sunbeam,
> Jesus wants me for a sunbeam.
> I'll be a sunbeam for Him.

Chapter 16

Whenever I could, I followed my uncle around, watching his every move. I sat next to him as he rested in his bed away from the afternoon heat. As the pulse on his arm beat a steady rhythm, I wondered why mine didn't pulsate as well. He let me sit as close as I wanted to on his bed.

Here he differed from my father. With Father, you waited until he prompted the touch. He maintained a stern space around him, always working or on edge about something.

Uncle Mack opened one eye to peek at me. He cracked one of his irresistible laughs.

"A boy is a fart," he chuckled.

He closed his eye and rolled over to the other side. I took his reference to flatulence to mean relief. A fresh relief that brought humor to pent up feelings around our house. The sort of relief ushered in by the innocence of a child watching the ways of an ol' man.

Uncle renamed me "Buck Forehead" because of my prominent forehead. Like my father, I hated nicknames, but Uncle's playfulness allowed him to get away with calling me names. When my siblings tried to do the same, we fought a bitterly. Soon they, too, got their own nickname from the impartial uncle.

I got even with Uncle Mack when he made the mistake of claiming my pretend girlfriend to be his.

"All the girls have a right to follow Mack," he sang and danced as he claimed my pretend girl.

"You are an ol' man. You'll soon be dead," I shot back.

Uncle Mack got quiet and pensive. I felt the power of my victory, but I soon regretted my harsh statement as he seemed so hurt and defenseless. Quickly, he perked up and shot back.

"A boy is a fart."

His laughter shook the glass doors on the china cabinet in the living room and filled our lives with mirth. The hills outside echoed his delight, and it became pleasant in our valley.

"All the girls have a right to follow Mack."

It was good to hear him sing again. His warmth spread from our home to everyone. He called the young men "brother-in-law" and won their affection. They were flattered that he considered marrying their sister and going beyond friendship to be an "in-law."

He worked his magic daily on a group of construction workers passing our home to build a two-story mansion for the local grocer, Miss Mattie. As the caravan of trucks passed, the men called for Uncle Mack.

"Brother-in-law, brother-in-law," they sang, and stopped the trucks until he showed his face and waved at the crowd.

The hardened faces of the men lit up and made the valley a magical place to be. Soon they shortened the greeting to "bro-'n-law, bro-'n-law." As my brother and I watched, the men began calling us "bro-'n-law" too. When Mamma came to observe the celebrations, the men clapped and shouted.

"Sister-'n-law, sister-'n-law." Mamma smiled and waved cheerfully.

Father did not join the merriment. He never frowned on it either. As protector and provider for a wife and four children, he kept up his guard. The men would just as soon challenge his control of the family. Most days when the caravan passed, he was away in the fields hoeing weeds.

Chapter 17

One Saturday, a powerful afternoon thunderstorm swept into our neighborhood and drove us inside for shelter. Rain flew sideways in huge, white, puffy sheets. The ackee tree flailed about in the wind. Hail pounded the zinc roof. Fearing the storm might blow off the roof, I awakened Uncle Mack from his nap.

An active hurricane season left my family on edge. This unease began before Uncle Mack came from Cuba. A huge hurricane, Hurricane Flora, threatened to run over the island. We feared that the hurricane might blow down our old house.

During the day, our parents listened to the weather bulletin on the little transistor radio. Father's lips were tighter than usual, and Mamma barely spoke. We were in the middle of the growing season, and the deluge could possibly destroy our crops. Before sunset, Mamma sent my sister Jan to bring in the garments that were hanging on the clothesline.

Jan ran back inside, covering her face, and crying as if she had witnessed something dreadful. Tears flowed freely past her fingers.

Mamma and I hurried to determine what alarmed her. Jan pointed in the direction of the approaching storm. An unusual image clung menacingly to the sky as the setting sun touched the high cirrus clouds. Blood-red clouds with brighter yellow bands cut across the sky. Gone were the softer blue colors that made a rainbow pleasing to behold. The reflection looked like a gruesome ladder drawn in blood. No amount of reassurance from our parents calmed our fears of the lucid omen.

Despite our fears, Hurricane Flora missed the island at the last minute. Some say the Blue Mountain to the east of the island deflected the storm away from the people. Our house survived, and the storm spared our crops.

My fear of storms resurged as I watched this afternoon tempest toss the branches outside our house. I touched my uncle's arm. He awakened from his nap.

"Uncle Mack," I pleaded, "can you cut the storm outside?"

Previously, I overheard him telling Mamma that when he lived in Cuba, he once cut the power of a storm by praying and commanding the winds to cease. My uncle enjoyed a kind of sainthood. He avoided drinking and smoking, and his "love thy neighbor attitude" fostered his exalted reputation.

He seemed bored with my request, but I persisted. Finally, he sat up in bed and mumbled a few words in Spanish. He closed his eyes and resumed his nap. I expected him to wave his arms at the storm and cause the rain to trickle to a few drops. He napped peacefully. I waited.

The storm still lashed out in fury, pouring solid walls of water into the wind. I prayed, but nothing could cut its power.

Chapter 18

"You have to go to Chuch o' Christ," Father commanded every Sunday.

I practically grew up in the church by the crossroad. My parents rarely attended, but they made sure that I did. The first time I sat on the wooden benches, my feet were too short to touch the floor. I marked off the years sitting and praying for my shoes to reach the concrete floor like the teenagers. Before long, I knew all the hymns in the songbook and the Bible stories from the sermons.

One Sunday, three white American missionaries showed up for services. Parson Brown, the local elder, grinned from ear to ear as he welcomed them. He stood up to preach at the pulpit when suddenly he thudded to the floor and remained motionless.

A known epileptic, he had experienced other seizures in the community, but nobody expected him to fall in the house of the Lord. A hush fell over the church. Women fanned themselves with songbooks and the air thickened with fear. The missionary men took off their coats and knelt on the hard-concrete floor next to the elder. They took turns praying for him to "rise and walk."

Judging by the length of their prayers, they professed more faith than the locals. Normally, folks placed a cushion under the head of a fallen epileptic's skull, stuck a spoon in his mouth, and waited for the spell to pass.

Parson Brown's hands clung rigidly to his side. From where I sat on the high wooden bench, the Parson's brown wing- tip shoes pointed skyward as if in supplication. The missionaries kept praying, and we waited for something to happen.

Tales of Elder Brown's rugged strength filled village folklore. He used his jaw strength to lift a burlap bag filled with one hundred pounds of corn grains. Though he had fallen many times before, he appeared unscarred.

Suddenly, the elder bounced to his feet. He smiled profusely and tried to reassure us. The missionaries slowly rose from the long hours of praying. Among them, a tall young man kept flicking back his long hair from his face. His brow wrinkled with compassion for the elder.

I knew the names of all the missionaries since my sisters described the men to me. My sisters attended church summer camp with the missionaries, and the girls expressed how the missionaries made camp so much fun. Hazel mentioned that the tall man often played the guitar and sang for them at campfire. His guitar case remained unopened as they watched over Parson Brown. I wished he would play.

Two of the men sat on either side of the elder lest he fall out again. The spell of illness departed from him for a season. They refused to let him preach anymore that day.

Nobody in the church thought to comfort us, the young children. We were still holding our breaths.

Chapter 19

The following Sunday, Uncle Buster strode to the church podium, squared his shoulders, and stroked the flawless wooden pulpit. His eyes measured every face before he raised his hand. The congregation fell silent. Light from the afternoon sun filtered through the glass window behind him and lit the platform. Though only a deacon, Uncle electrified the congregation much more than Elder Brown could.

Every opportunity Uncle got, he preached about sinful people who repented and converted to Christianity. He spoke frequently about Saul, a notorious persecutor of early Christians.

Saul "breathed out murderous threats" and set out on his horse to attack Christians. A light (Shekinah) from heaven struck Saul from his steed, blinding him. Saul repented, changed his name to Paul, and became Christianity's most ardent evangelist.

"Shine the Shekinah light on the church today," Uncle preached.

A chorus of "Praise the Lord" echoed his call. Our doctrine forbade people from getting in the spirits, and the leaders taught us to utter a more reserved "Praise the Lord."

"For to worship. For to worship," I snickered and elbowed my friend Ronny sitting next to me on the church bench. We knew Uncle's next tale.

Uncle told the unlikely story of how the Ethiopian eunuch converted to Christianity. He loved conversions. Uncle's sermons seemingly asked atonement for past transgressions that he would never admit to. He was an infamous womanizer, but nobody admitted to that kind of sin in church.

Uncle ignored our snickering. Despite his strained relationship with my father, he warmed to me. He should learn my name and stop calling me "Young Gil" after my father, Gilbert. He said I looked like Father, but I wanted none of my father's sins.

"Shall we pray?"

Uncle asked a church sister in the congregation to offer the closing prayer. Her soprano voice bridged prayer and song as she pleaded for her dying mother.

"Lawd, comfort my mother before she departs on the journey where travelers go and no message return. Be with her as death lays its icy hands on her."

A stir of emotions rippled through the congregation. One of the members, the local barber, caught the spirit and began to animate his trance. Still seated, his hands flew violently in the air, and his tie flipped upright on its own accord. His shoulders unhinged and rotated backward. His face twitched to the same rhythm that made his shoulders bounce. With his lips pursed, he emitted a shrill wail that made even the stoic parson cringe. The barber's actions set off other members, who began their own high-pitched wails. By the sound of it, half the church joined him.

Where was the normally calm barber who often came to our house to trim my brother's and my hair? Back then, he sat me under the shade of the sweet-sap tree next to our house and pointed his long scissors at my head. He trimmed the curls close to my skull. Next, he used a razor to shave my hairlines into the latest styles. The man cut meticulously with the blade. He never nicked my skin or twitched uncontrollably.

Whatever moved him to act bizarre in church filled me with fear. Tears flowed down my face, and the ever-observant Sunday school teacher caught me mopping my eyes with my sleeves. A quizzical frown crossed her brow.

"Why you crying, Dan-Dan?"

Her question baffled me. She should be weeping as well. A peculiar thing just took over our church.

I felt the "spirit" that the church sister evoked with her prayer, but I would never to admit that. Crying carried a lesser penalty. At nine years old, I preferred being called soft rather than a boy who *got in the spirit*. Folks caught up in the spirit were fodder for gossip at the village crossroads.

"Ronny pinched me," I lied.

The Sunday school teacher looked tenderly at Ronny, her cousin, and rolled her eyes in disbelief at me. The boy would harm nobody, but she put her arms around me until I calmed down.

Normally, Uncle Buster would shake his head indignantly when people "got in the spirit," quaking, and hollering during service. He was an outspoken man, but, surprisingly, he never voiced his sentiments. He appeared torn between breaking up the proceedings and skipping out the door to his home nearby, but he chewed his lip and kept quiet. Fortunately, the white missionaries did not come to church that day. They would surely have frowned on this unsanctioned behavior.

The trance waned to a few sporadic twitches from the barber. He became the neat, composed man who came to our house to trim my hair. As Parson Brown concluded the services, Uncle tossed his hat to his balding dome. He skipped the formal parting and cut a path across the lawn to his home next door. Church ran on too long, and he had no tolerance for hunger, or people "getting in the spirit."

Chapter 20

Cousin Cedric trotted his white donkey past the church at the crossroad to visit us from Wanstead, a village six miles back in the woodlands. He sat with Father under our "good-for-nothing" mango tree that only bore maggot-laden fruits. The men talked for hours as they rolled homegrown tobacco into long cigars.

"Dan-Dan, go bring me a fire-stick."

I ran to the kitchen for a glowing twig to light their cigars. They puffed contentedly. A rare smile swiped at the wrinkles on Father's face. He seemed to stop wrestling with his worries. The smell of tobacco comforted me, a peace offering to troubled lives.

Flecks of gold sparkled on Cedric's dentures as Mamma handed him a wedge of homemade sweet-potato pudding. As he bit into the gummy pastry, I feared it might wrench his dentures from his gum. Happily, his false teeth held, and he grinned in delight. No one baked a sweet-potato pudding like Mamma's.

Cedric came to see Aunt Edith, Father's older sister, who returned home after living in the United States for decades. She moved in with a truckload of chests laden with glimpses of the American lifestyle. She spoke like an educated American and insisted we drop the local patois around her.

"Oh, he convinces me with his smile, like an evangelist," she cooed and named me *the Evangelist*.

Like Uncle Mac, she possessed a knack for naming people, but I wished she named me *the Senator,* the label she assigned my brother Serge. Secretly, I wanted to be a powerful politician, but she gave the coveted title to my brother, the instinctive manipulator. From her forty years of caring for wealthy people's kids in New York, she knew how to gauge children's character.

My aunt instructed Cousin Alonzo to build a bookcase, and she stocked it with encyclopedias and novels. We owned one of the largest collections of books in the mountains.

She also brought several portraits to decorate our walls. One showed a boy about my age alertly saluting a man of immense presence. The picture, Auntie fondly explained, showed John-John saluting his father, the deceased American president, John Kennedy.

A portrait of my uncle who had passed away many years previously glowered back at President Kennedy. This uncle too held a strong military bearing. Father explained that it was a portrait of his oldest brother, Luther, who served in World War I. Uncle Luther shaved off his wavy curls to pass for white and then joined the Navy. While in the Navy, a service man found him out and called him a nigger. Uncle smashed the other man's face with his fist.

Father clenched his fist into angry missiles and thumped the air, siding with Luther as he told the tale. His arms rippled with muscles hardened from a lifetime of labor. Hard work fostered the family claim of being equal to anybody.

Uncle's portrait stared back at me from the wall. With his hair trimmed close to the skull, he might easily "pass for white." Father mumbled that Uncle Luther "was gravely wounded" when the Germans torpedoed his boat. The faces on the wall seemed far away in another world embroiled with the conflicts of race and color.

"Your poor hands," Aunt Edith broke in as she clasped Cedric's hand. Her favorite cousin's palm felt coarser than sandpaper. She took a bottle of olive oil from her chest and massaged his hands.

"Why Auntie is doing this to me, eh?" Cedric protested halfheartedly.

He kept smiling as she emptied the bottle in a vain attempt to make his hands soft and supple.

On his regular visits, Cousin Cedric always grasped my hand in his giant fist and stroked my palm reassuringly. His coarse hands triggered the sensation of walking barefoot across a pile of rock stones, but I felt safe in his rough grasp. His were the hands of a man who worked hard to feed his family.

Before he left, Cedric shook my hand again. Aunt Edith's olive oil failed to soften his hands. His palm remained rougher than sandpaper. I knew that genteel hands were useless to grasp the lifeless handle of a pickaxe and worthless on the hardwood grip of a hoe. Soft hands were unfit to wield the heavy steel balanced in a machete.

The donkey trotted off, and Cedric's long legs occasionally scraped the ground. Mama called out the traveler's blessing.

"Walk good!"

A few months later, news arrived from Wanstead that my cousin was on his deathbed.

"Lawd God, Dan-Dan, you have to go with me to look for Cedric," Father snapped.

As he prepared for the long trudge, I saw Father use a cane for the first time. I hoped that the idea of a walking stick just was a fashion statement. Only helpless ol' men plodded along with a cane, not my father.

The road to Wanstead climbed up a rocky roadway meandering through hillsides overflowing with leafy trees. People stopped work to greet us. These were sturdy farmers, but everyone knew of Father's reputation for hard work. The men craved his company, and he obliged, stopping to share tobacco that he grew in the valley below our house.

Father propped one leg against a rock wall and rolled a cigar on his thigh. Usually he whisked about hastily, but when he rolled his cigar, he deliberately formed a perfect cylinder, and sealed it with a slow lick from his lips. Time stopped while they smoked.

The men rarely spoke, sharing some common, silent tongue. They never asked why we trudged along a road that dead-ended in the remote hills. They seem to know we were going to bid farewell to Cousin Cedric before he left on a journey where travelers go, and no messages return.

Father took a break to see a man named Sam Manning. Anyone who bore that last name was our cousin. Sam Manning had gone through death's door and back. He still suffered from a strange stomach affliction that left him shadow-thin.

His shirt hung loosely, and his belt struggled to hold his trousers to his meager waist. A smile tried to light his face. Years younger than Father, he looked beaten and too frail to be outdoors.

"Poor fellow," Father muttered to himself. He told me they worked side-by-side in a munition's factory during World War II. Even then, Sam often became ill. We plodded on.

Cars or busses never attempted to navigate these steep hillsides. A truck crept down the slopes carrying fruits for the juice factory in the plains. Jackasses, laden with yams, hustled toward the village square to meet the country bus that hauled their produce to town.

Father used his bamboo cane sparingly, and he seemed unsure about how to employ it. I hoped he would burn it in the morning fire next day when he made coffee. Bamboo made the best kindling for a fire gone cold. I could not reconcile the image of my father as an ol' man leaning on a walking stick.

We climbed countless hills and saw few valleys until the road ended and we trudged across a small plateau to Cousin Cedric's house. The men in our family all knew how to nurture life from the soil. All around, the crops grew lush and vigorous.

Cedric's wife had returned to her family in the plains a long time ago. She took their only surviving daughter with her because none of their other five children survived the primal conditions in Wanstead. Cedric lived in a small two-bedroom house with a woman named Miss Vin. The woman had gone past the role of lover to become his nurse.

Miss Vin wore a brightly colored red-and-white plaid bandana, the kind used by women like Ma Ann to keep their hair private. Her exaggerated curves told the story of a woman reshaped by pregnancy, breastfeeding, and child-rearing. Cousin Cedric often spoke of their warm relationship. She greeted us anxiously, explaining that the doctor had given up on Cousin Cedric.

A gentle breeze blew through the plateau, flipping the lush banana leaves to reveal their pale, vulnerable undersides. Through the open door, I saw Cousin Cedric's long form stretched on his bed. He could glimpse the crops in the fields where his labor made the land fruitful. Miss Vin left the door open for the dying man.

"Uncle Gil." He greeted Father with hoarseness just about a whisper.

Father climbed the two stone steps to the room and took a seat on the chair by the bed. The men sat in silence as usual, only this time they did not spit or smoke hand-rolled cigars.

"Where's Dan-Dan?" Cousin Cedric croaked. Father motioned me inside.

Halfheartedly, I climbed up the cut-stone steps and walked across the bulletwood floor. Not even a peace offering of hand-rolled cigars could remove the smell of sickness and death in the house.

The clean floor appeared worn from a lifetime of use. The red soil in these limestone hills is relentless. It stained the wood and covered the dark annual rings characteristic of bulletwood. Lacking the energy to grasp my hand and reassure me with his coarse grip, Cousin just tried to smile.

He started coughing, and Miss Vin held up the white enamel chamber pot for him to spit out a heavy discharge of mucus. She patiently fed him teaspoons of lime juice and honey, her last remedy for his lung cancer. I waited for the concoction to bring a smile to his face as it always did when Mamma gave me this tonic for my cold. Cedric's coughing ceased, but the smile never came to his face.

He stretched his long form on the bed, and his usual calm poise returned. Miss Vin took Father on a walk away from the house. Out of my earshot, she spoke, and Father listened with unusual quietness. They met briefly, heads lowered, voices low, away from a curious child. Father asked something about cedar boards. That meant nothing to me.

A woman back in my church often prayed that people on their deathbed might find strength for a journey where travelers go, and messages never return. I wished I could tell my cousin to walk good on his journey, but the words stuck in my throat. I longed for the warmth of his gravelly hands on mine.

We left Cousin Cedric listening to the breeze blowing through the banana plants. He stared past the yam vines wrapping tall bamboo poles resisting the wind. The harvest should be good this year, but he would reap no more White Afu yams from the fields.

Father's lips clamped tight on the long walk home. Though he never declared it, I knew he loved his cousin. I knew what my father was thinking. Sometimes he wondered aloud if he would be around to see the children come of age. Cousin Cedric was almost two decades younger than Father's seventy years.

By the time we got the news that Cousin Cedric had passed away, they had already buried him. News came slowly from the distant woods in Wanstead, and they had no way to keep a corpse preserved. Father never spoke of Cedric again, but I knew he missed his friend and the times they spent rolling cigars under the good-for-nothing mango tree.

Chapter 21

About five years after they buried his mother under the cedar trees, Sonny returned from the big city. He just showed up beside as I walked through the crossroads on the way to school. At first, I didn't connect the "new Sonny" to the helpless boy at his mother's funeral. This Sonny spoke with the confidence of a city slicker. In his brown lace-up shoes and city clothes, he stood out as someone of high breeding.

At times, he attracted the fury of other children who envied his style. His clothes never bothered me. City shoes don't last long on our rocky trails. Soon he hobbled around barefooted like the rest of us.

By then, I understood the dark secret behind the fence at Sonny's yard. Away from the ear of the adults, older children gossiped in hushed voices. Sonny and his siblings were products of incest. Their father, Isaiah, had taken his niece to be the mother of ten children.

My father always warned us to keep the ram goats away from their female siblings. Rams zestfully mated even with their close relatives. A "near blood" mating resulted in stunted, deformed progeny.

Sonny appeared to have shaken off the shadows that his family hid behind the large trees at their gate. He seemed as well adjusted as any other child. We became good friends, and daily we walked with a trail of boys to the elementary school.

Soon, Sonny outdid most country boys at their own tricks. He mastered the use of the slingshot and shot more birds than I ever could. He also knew the name of every tree from the tropical hardwood forest in our backyards.

Deftly, he handled a machete like a grown man. With his left hand, a blur of speed, he carved figures from the hardest wood. I attempted to impress him with my outdoor skills by opening coconut with a rock. I lifted the rock and dropped it on the coconut. The rock bounced off and landed on my bare feet splitting my middle toe. The nail and muscle hung off the bone. I shuffled on my heels for home. Sonny treaded silently beside me, wearing alarm on his face.

Mamma patched me up without giving me hell for causing my own injury. She touched my cheek with her open hand, checking my temperature.

"You have a fever," she pronounced and confined me to bed.

The fever subsided, but my lame toe mended slowly. When my wound healed, the muscle grew sideways off the bone and the nail struggled to regrow. I limped back to school with Sonny at my side.

Chapter 22

At ten years old, our dog Rally should have been too old for the hunt, but neither Rally nor Father ever slowed down much with age. Rally and Castro chased a mongoose back into the rocks above our house, and Father followed with his iron bar. Alerted by the ruckus, a neighbor brought his dog to the hunt. The dog, a short, muscular hound with a stump for a tail, constantly challenged Rally to lead the hunt. Rally kept him in place with a chilling snarl.

The mongoose refused to budge from the rocks. The neighbor set a fire next to the rock wall to smoke out the prey. Quickly, the smoke billowed up and ferreted out the pest. Rally sprang to its head, but the mongoose snapped quicker than his aging skills. Rally jumped back and yelped as the mongoose bit him on his face. Castro, his faithful companion, leapt to the rescue and captured the quarry.

Rally overcame the initial shock and joined the kill. The dogs left their catch intact, refusing to rip it apart as they were accustomed to. Father poked the mongoose with the iron bar, flipping it over as he marveled at its ferocity.

Rally crawled under the cellar and stayed away from us. I felt sad to see the family's best friend so withdrawn. He recovered slowly from the bite, and I wondered if he might ever be the same hunting dog that grew up with us.

When he healed, Rally reverted to one of his territorial instincts of chasing the grocery truck as it drove past. Mamma always warned us to stop Rally from following us when the truck passed, but the faithful dog accompanied us every time we left home. One day, the truck hit Rally and Chang, the driver, sped away.

Rally's face held more than pain as he limped back home. He seemed shocked that his normally agile limbs had failed him. For many years, he skipped around the tires of the truck barking and chasing it away from us. His face also showed sorrow that he failed to protect us from the truck interrupting our lives with its loud motor grinding up the hill.

Rally crawled back to the cellar where he could hear the lively voices of four children above him. He whimpered quietly, rested his head on his paws, and his eyes gazed at some unseen, distant object. Elderly folks stricken with "ol' age sickness," had this same look as they waited for death to come calling.

In a few days, Rally was gone. Father buried him underneath a small cedar tree and placed a rock where he laid his head. The John-Crows came to the cedar tree because they did not hear his bark anymore.

One morning on the way to school, Gene called out excitedly to me. The crows were kneeling on the branches of the cedar tree as if praying. Crows normally devoured corpses, but my cousin felt that the birds came to pay their last respect to the best dog that ever-set foot in our village. Even though Rally had previously bitten Gene, my cousin knew the right words to comfort us. Mamma fought back tears as she informed Gene of Rally's last stand.

When Chang drove by to make deliveries the following week, Mamma told the driver that he killed our dog. To placate her, he promised to bring her a replacement dog.

"Me bring you good dog. Good dog," he reassured in his Jamaican Chinese accent.

He never brought any dog. He had taken the life of a legend, and that is irreplaceable.

Part 2: Scorpions of the Crossroad

Chapter 23

Four roads crisscrossed the hillsides and intersected at the village square. Four shops, each with its own history embedded in hurricane battered roofs, stood at the corners. The junction marked the only port of entry to the area, and everything happened there. Folks trekked from beyond the hills and valleys to purchase household supplies or to get mail from the post office. On the weekends, they trudged through the piazza to hear the word of God in one of the churches.

To win votes at election time, the local politician ordered the roads at the intersection paved with asphalt. His crews spread marl and gravel over the rest of the hillside roads. By the end of the rainy season the gravel washed into the gullies, and water rushing down the slopes cut patches in the asphalt. The politician won the contest and dropped out of sight until the next election five years later.

Miss Mattie's two-story building hosted the most up-to-date business in the piazza. In front of her store, Jacob, the best tailor in our area, sewed trousers at the other end of the butcher shop.

Across from the butcher, a two-story shop from a bygone era towered over the square. A succession of business people operated the store and then moved on. The weathered shop kept the name, Mister Chin Shop, for the best grocer who ran that business. *Bygone Days* might be a more fitting name for the shop. Anything you bought from that shop smelled musty with age. Only scorpions crept around in those shadowy conditions.

Folklore said that ghosts could not pass through the intersection where the roads cut across the hills to form a cross. The powerful symbol of the cross blocked evil spirits. Not a soul ever saw a ghost at the intersection, but the symbolic cross could not stop vile men from haunting the square and tormenting the unlucky passersby.

Drunks spewed bile daily from the rum bar. Idlers waited there to poke fun at the local man who took a trip into mania. If good things happened at the intersection, nobody remembered.

The new prime minister, Mr. Singer, came through our village, and folks dressed in their Sunday clothes to meet him at the square. People from opposing political persuasions gathered without reservation. Father hated the crossroad. He detested the idlers there. He bought his goods at the shops and swiftly returned home. The novelty of the prime minister's visit made Father shed his reservations. He led his children to the community square.

He lined up all four of us against the coarse cement wall at one of the old shops. He placed us in birth order. Hazel, the oldest, went first, standing tall and strong at the head of the line. Next, Jan, then me, while Serge, the youngest, shuffled at the end of the line. My family waited with the discipline of an honor guard to see the prime minister. Mamma stayed home.

Whenever a conflict broke out at the crossroad, Money-Roy or his sister Treetop initiated it. Treetop positioned herself in the middle of the road. Her legs, sturdy as hardwood timber, stretched above my head. She pulled her daughter, a girl slightly younger than my nine years, by the hand. The child kicked her shoes defiantly on the ground, squirmed in her pink dress, and tried to escape. Treetop dragged her back to the front of the crowd and bellowed.

"Me a go beg Mass Singer some money."

Most people knew how to string together a few words in formal English for such an occasion. Treetop only spoke the local Patois. Her voice rumbled with the thunder of a storm heading over the mountains to our valley.

The prime minister stepped from the car with an air of assertiveness. He looked more at ease in a jacket than any man I knew. By comparison, men in my church were well-dressed scarecrows in their ill-fitting Sunday jackets.

With one long step, Treetop cut him off and rumbled.

"Mass Singer me a beg you some money. See mi daughta deh, don't even have on any slip."

We gasped as Treetop raised the girl's dress to show the missing undergarment. Without breaking stride or vocalizing, Mr. Singer reached inside his jacket and fished out a coin. He displayed an English two-and-six piece, with a value of twenty-five pennies. He dropped the hefty coin into her open palm and moved on without haste. For an instant, his face almost showed disgust, but he masked his sentiments and kept pace.

Father kept us pressed to the wall away from the crude conflict. We were better than this woman bringing her shame to the crossroad. Miss Mattie, the shopkeeper, opened the counter and led Mr. Singer away from the press of people. Locals never crossed to the other side of the grocery shop.

Long after the prime minister left, Treetop clutched her coin, clasping, and unclasping her fist. She stared at the piece. I expected her usual stream of expletives to fill the crossroad, but she seemed torn between the weight of the coin and its meager value. The money might buy bread, but it couldn't purchase the slip she needed for her daughter. The little girl escaped to seek anonymity in the crowd.

For once, Money-Roy remained quiet as he failed to find a way to make fun of my family. Father ushered us home. He detested the people who loitered like ghosts at the crossroad.

Chapter 24

Grand Market remained the one night when my father gave in and took us to celebrate at the piazza. The roots of Grand Market date to the island's colonial past when the masters gave their slaves one day off to commemorate Christmas Eve. Folks released their pent-up feelings in one long night of merrymaking. Grand Market turn into the most festive holiday in the nation.

On this night, we were closest as a family. Father dropped his tense personality, and Mamma's smile reassured us that we should relax and have a good time. Customers filled all four shops at the corners, happily buying last minute gift for Christmas.

Older teens romped in the square. Light from the kerosene lanterns spilled from the shops into the crossroad. Electricity power lines never made it over the mountains to power our homes. The teens lit the short fuse on their starlight flares and tossed them as high as possible into the night sky. The starlight flares illuminated the night sky and then arched downward trailing sparkles to the earth. Everyone cheered until darkness swallowed the flare.

By the side of the road, youngsters crowded around the Crown and Anchor gambling tables. The banker at one of the tables raised his leather cup filled with dice. He shook it at the sky. *Klup-klup*, the dice rattled back at the man. He waved the youngsters on, prodding them to fish out more coins and gamble. The youngsters placed their bets, clinking coins to the table.

A torch fashioned from a glass soda bottle filled with kerosene oil lighted each table. The torches drew tall shadows of the figures crowding around the gambling board. Barry Davis, one of the bankers at the tables, eyed everyone with glassy, suspicions eyes. Occasionally, Barry inverted the bottle to moisten the newspaper wick with kerosene. The torch flared up and spilled a trail of burning liquid to the ground. If this fluid dribbled on the feet of a careless child, that toe might be set aflame, but at Grand Market, everyone wore shoes.

Jacob was in a good mood in his tailor shop. He finished sewing men's trousers for the festive season and collected a pocket full of money. He took elaborate pains to prepare his Coleman lantern. At a snail's pace, he filled it with kerosene oil, and then slowly pumped it with air before he lit it. The Coleman gave off bright white light unlike the smoky lamp we used to illuminate our house.

Next, he prepared the iron he used to press clothes. He owned the only fancy pressing iron in our area. Mama always used the clumsy flat irons that she heated on a bed of hot charcoal. She pressed for a few minutes until the iron ran cool and then heated them again.

Jacob filled the iron with charcoal and added pieces of cotton fabric. Deliberately he touched a match to the cloth. It would be faster to use kerosene to light the charcoal, but he seemed to enjoy tinkering with the fire. When the charcoal glowed, Jacob fiddled with the latch before closing it. Finally, he placed it on his pressing table. He worked slower than the evening shadows creeping over the square. People left Jacob to his toil and joined the festivity at the crossroad.

Reputed to be a palm reader, Jacob hardly ever got work telling fortunes in the village square. Most people accepted their fate to live in our narrow valley caught up between the hills. You had to leave to change your fortune. He could weave a tale to last all night, and Mamma enjoyed listening to him. Father had no such indulgences. He scorned people who talked too much and took too long to get work done.

Amid the activities, Mamma called out in alarm.

"Look, look, a running star."

She pointed to the falling star streaking over the hill and heading to the square. Light flew in all directions as it fell, but the star persisted. It kept alight until tree level, and then it burst into a thousand pieces and lit up the tall trumpet tree above the square. I saw the green color of the huge leaves as the burning pieces illuminated the night. The huge leaves, suspended on long stems, reached toward the sky like many pairs of palms turned upwards praying for mercy. The flaming trail fell halfway down the tree, and then everything went dark.

We knew all about the distress sign of a falling star. Mamma used this warning from the skies many times before. Someone would die tonight, unexpectedly. Father's voice lost its relaxed tone.

"Come!" he resounded. My siblings and I ran to him as chicks to the brood at the approach of a hawk. Hazel, the overprotective sibling, hovered over us, frowning.

We hurried home in silence. Father pointed the way with his flashlight. He slipped on a gray pullover that Mamma had stitched together for him from an old sweater that someone sent to us from America. We huddled closer seeking comfort from the chilly north winds.

When we turned onto the stony path that led to our home, we heard running feet and panicked voices. The neighbor's older teenage boys were fleeing home. They were always playing pranks, and we paid them no mind. Father pushed open the unlocked door and motioned us inside. Our parents said nothing of their thoughts as they urged us to bed.

In the morning, early to rise as ever, Father got the news first. Right after we left the crossroad, someone cut the throat of Buffington, the local bully. Blood spilled all over the crossroad.

We ate the black fruitcake that Mamma made and sipped the warm homemade eggnog with breakfast. I tried to understand the tragedy that occurred in our young lives. Mamma made the best black fruitcake, and it softened the memory of the horrible night.

Our parents kept us away from the square for the rest of that Christmas break, but the following January we passed through the crossroad on the way to school. The blood-red paint marks left by the crime scene detectives told the tale of where the knife slit Buffington's throat.

More paint trailed drops of blood as Buffington ran toward the light of Mister Chin's shop. The detectives outlined a human form where he fell with legs splayed east to west at the crossroad. One of the older boys plopped down in the outline, grasped his throat, and quivered, mimicking the death throes of the fallen man. A tremor ran down my spine. I slipped away.

Everyone in the village knew that Buffington, a bull of a man, could easily destroy any fellow in single combat. The day before Buffington's murder he bullied Barry Davis, the crown-and-anchor man, chasing him off the road. Davis sneaked home through the back roads of Foga Woods and, with his brother, devised a method to slay Buffington.

Not one person came forward to testify during the trials, but Braman, the Rasta man, never kept quiet.

"You know who killed Buffington?"

Out of fear of reprisal from Barry Davis's family, no one replied.

"I know." His eyes twinkled.

"Death kill him to blood bath."

The smell of blood shattered the innocence of the children left at the crossroad that night, but Mamma's alarm saved us from witnessing the carnage. On the way through the piazza, I stepped around the detective's paint marks outlining where Buffington fell. It took years before the bloody paint marks faded enough for me to feel safe to go barefooted on the path that traced his bloody fall.

The shopkeeper tried to reopen Mr. Chin's shop after Buffington's bloodstains faded, but nobody went inside to buy his goods. He eventually barricaded the building and left. Duck ants (termites) slowly wasted it away. A man explained the speeding decline of the building. He believed that if people we not living in the building and breathing on the walls every day, duck ants would invade the structure and eat the beams to the ground.

As the duck ants built their tunnels through the beams, the decaying shop reminded folks of the village's lost innocence. Everyone longed to see it go. Bit by bit, one of the local lads flattened the decaying shop to its foundations. He pounded the structure with a long bulletwood pole to release the energy that beset him on his many dark cruises into mania.

Chapter 25

The murder at the village square gave me more reason to detest the idlers and drunks at the crossroad bar. At the rum bar, drunken men belched their fury into the air. What made these men so angry? Would I become like them?

I refused to accompany my sister Jan to the grocery shop on Saturdays. Father whirled his belt and chased me up the hill behind our house. I easily outran his aging legs, but I stopped in my tracks when Mamma's heartbroken plea rang out.

"Dan-Dan, you want me to send you to 'formatory school?"

She knew better than placing me with the bad boys at the reformatory school in the big city. Just to placate Mamma, I followed my sister to the square.

On the way home, what appeared to be a passing afternoon shower would not abate. We ran to the shelter of the post office verandah. Rain blew sideward on huge gusts of blustering wind, drenched our flimsy clothes, and pooled on the verandah floor. The deluge gushed from clouds high above our peaks with a cold fury.

We should have noticed the build-up of the storm as the afternoon sun drove moisture upward to form dark, brooding, cumulonimbus clouds. Ol' folks said if we listened carefully, we might feel the updraft of moist air rushing up to build a storm. If we were attentive, we would have heard the distant thunder, high up in the clouds, rumbling angrier than the men drinking at the bar. The dogs moping near shelter ought to have alerted us of imminent danger.

A man dressed in a khaki outfit sheltered in the weather-beaten verandah. He staked claim to the driest spot on the porch, and we shuffled around him, trying to keep our bare feet out of the pools of water on the verandah floor. His clothes looked new and clean, as if he never spent a day digging dirt like most men. When he moved, his black rubber boots smacked his thighs. Father wore similar boots when he worked in the fields on a wet day.

The man staked out a corner of the verandah, talking to the postmistress. He lived in the big city for a while, and his city twang showed off his superior standing. From the stony look in his eyes, I knew he disliked children. He seemed annoyed that my sister and I interrupted their conversation.

I knew the woman used every opportunity to preach her religious zeal. She once visited our house to convert my father to her church. On the cover of the magazine that graced her lap, a serpent offered an enticing red apple to Eve. She argued that a serpent tempted Eve to unleash original sin in the Garden of Eden. Father cut her off.

"Only a man can tempt a woman."

The postmistress smiled uncomfortably. She stuffed her magazine in a polished leather bag and bolted to her post office. She should not have even dreamed of converting Father. He simply believed in hard work and sometimes praying for rain to grow his yams.

From her dry, secure position behind the burglar bars of the post office, she eyed us shuddering in the rain-drenched porch. A streak of blue lightning sliced the air and struck the post office box with a metallic ping. A shock of electricity zipped through the wet floor, jolted me, and shook my knees. Gasping, I writhed away from the opening and pressed up against the rough facade of the cement wall. The lightning and the furious downpour trapped us in the waterlogged verandah.

Repeatedly lightning flashed, the mailbox pinged, and I felt the jolt. The shock reminded me of the fearful black scorpion in the latrine and its dreadful stinger threatening to sting my arse. Hailstones bounced pebbles around on the road, cutting off any possible escape.

If there was thunder, I heard none of it. All conversation ceased. Again, and again, lightning pinged off the mailbox, etching tiny marks on the metal. Each successive ping rang in my ears. Unmoved, the man in khaki stayed in his adult world.

I prayed in my heart for the postmistress to offer us shelter since Jan and her niece were best friends. Instead, the indifferent woman marveled at the power of the storm and the frequency of the lightning strikes.

Finally, Jan muttered that she felt the shocks from the lightning spreading through the soaked floor. Unimpressed, the postmistress turned to the man.

"Mr. Michigan are you feeling it?"

"No, Miss McNeil."

She paused in thought.

"Why aren't you feeling it, Mr. Michigan?"

As an educated woman, she spoke better English than regular country folks. She never bothered to ask me how I felt, and I remained silent. In this adult world, nobody cared about children's emotions.

The man growled an insincere answer.

"I don't know, Miss McNeill. It must be because I am wet already." A smirk spread his perfectly manicured moustache past his cheeks. Another jolt zapped our bare feet as his insulated rubber boots protected him from the electrical shocks.

Why don't she invite us around to the back of her dry, safe world? I prayed. More lightning lit up the afternoon, and it finally gave the postmistress her divine cue.

"Come around to the back," she mumbled reluctantly.

Numb to the knees, I plunged alongside Jan into the rain. We ran through the metal gate and into the side door of the post office. The man in the black rubber boots bumped us in his rush for shelter. Apparently, he lost faith in the explanation that he was safe from lightning by being "wet already."

I fell into the only chair the postmistress offered, a rocking chair. My body let go, and I began to quake. I wrapped my arms around my knees to stop the tremors. The chair rocked with a mind of its own, broadcasting my plight.

Doggedly, the ping followed us. Lightning raced through the telegraph lines and pinged into the telegram machine. The device lit up as electrical energy discharged into the magnetic coil. Nobody talked.

The telegram machine stood dark and menacing on a neatly polished cedar table. The handle that the postmistress normally rotated to power the gadget sat frozen in place. I recalled watching the postmistress, on a dry day, frantically winding the handle and mouthing off the codes from a message.

"Dog, easy, able, dog,"

Jan told me that meant D-E-A-D. A neighbor had just died in the hospital in town far-far away, and there would be mourning in one of our homes.

Good news came slowly, never by the speedy telegraph. Occasionally, the postman brought a good news parcel with clothes from a relative in America. He carried the mail on his head, walking six miles from the junction at Cedars.

Water dripped from my soggy clothes onto the postmistress's highly polished cedar-wood flooring. I might be the first wet, barefooted boy to soil her floor. She had paid my sister's classmate good money to get on her knees and use a coconut brush to shine the boards.

"One time I tried crossing de bridge," the man growled, breaking the silence.

He spoke with a clever mix of the local Patois and English, like a city guy showing off. He told a story about a great storm in a faraway place. The river *come down*, overflowing its banks. He watched the currents sweeping the footbridge downstream. He slept on the riverbank that night. I wished he would cease his silly tale and focus on the great storm that was trying to kill me.

Even when the lightning abated, the air tingled with static energy. I felt like a magnet attracting lightning. Late in the evening, the rain let up enough for us to venture out. On shaking knees, I pushed the metal gate open, fully expecting to hear a ping and receive a jolt of electricity. Instead, the gate creaked to a close behind us.

I tested my feet on the litter of pebbles on the road. My limbs felt tender, but surprisingly they still worked. We set off for home. A light drizzle fell from black clouds following us. The normally green hillsides stood vexed and gray, resisting the dying sun's weak attempt to close the day with warmth.

We slipped into the house, afraid to tell anyone about our brush with lightning. We were afraid of adding more burdens to our parents. They always made me feel that I contributed to any possible mishap. Moreover, lightning struck and killed a parson in the next village as he preached at the pulpit. Not a single person ever survived a lightning strike.

Chapter 26

In time, I learned not to fear the post office and Buffington's bloody paint marks as I walked to the elementary school. At break time during my first year, a terrified bawling knifed through the air. I'd heard this cry before when a panicked ewe, tangled up to her throat in a brier vines, bleated for her life.

Families measure their economic worth by the number of goats they possess, and every part of the animal is used. The smell of curry goat-meat fills the air at all joyful events. Even my stern father began his day playfully toeing the black-and-white goatskin rug by his bed.

This bawl was not a goat's death cry, but a child's desperate plea. Nervously, I joined a semicircle of students jostling for space on the steps outside the principal's office. Tiptoeing, we took turns to peer over each other's shoulders.

"It's Betsy," hissed Mikey, one of my classmates. "I walked to school with her dis mawning."

Mikey pointed to the headmaster's desk on the elevated platform. I heard the incessant slap of leather on skin. A tall man, the headmaster's head towered above the crowd, his arm whirled, and the strap cut through the air like a black scorpion's tail. His eyes were riveted on his victim, but amid the torment, his face remained expressionless.

Another semicircle of students stood motionless by the desk, more lambs to the slaughter. I smelled fear, perhaps my own. Sweat doused my armpits and dribbled down my sides.

"That's Mr. Beastly, I hate dat man." Mikey furrowed his forehead, playing up his loathing.

The inner semicircle broke as Betsy came bawling through. Drops of urine formed perfect little circles on the dusty bulletwood floor, marking every step. Each drop dribbled smaller and smaller as she walked toward us. The trail marked the path from the headmaster's regal chair, down the steps, past our dust covered feet, and our sealed lips.

Her scrawny legs buckled as she wailed past us, but she steadied herself and plodded on. I wondered how Mr. Beastly found any flesh on her to beat. She was a bag-a-bones.

From beneath her long dress, brand new black shoes flicked out as she passed. Most of us watching only wore shoes on Sundays to church, but her father just returned from England with prestige. He was above sending a shoeless child to school.

In our silence, we sided with her and reviled the villain headmaster. The sound of her shoes pounded the floor, and the hollow cellar beneath the building echoed her footfalls. An empty silence followed her departure.

This was supposed to be a church-school. By the time a few elderly worshippers came to worship on Sunday, the urine stains would be gone.

A visiting minister from England often preached from the same platform where Mr. Beastly powered himself over the little girl. The visiting clergyman lectured about bloodstains and remission, but never about tortured children. As he preached, his Adam's apple bobbed like the drunk at the village rum bar. I wondered if the clergyman, too, craved a drink.

Chapter 27

The first time the headmaster slapped my face the violence and the senselessness of his action shocked me.

I sat obediently reading a book when I felt him towering over me. He shoved one foot on my desk, balanced an arm on his elevated thigh, and hovered, ready to strike. Sweat from my bare feet mingled with the red dust on the concrete floor. I glared at his polished black shoe as he fired a question at me. Before I answered, he grabbed the book and used it to slap my face.

Just as arrogantly, he dragged his foot off the desk, and the sound of his leather sole raked the air. He tossed the book back on my desk, pivoted, and exited the room. The odor of sweat and dirty feet tainted the air with fear. A principal is next to God in a tiny rural district.

For days, I watched the shoeprint on my desk and refused to wipe it away. In the scuffmarks, I saw the soul of the tortured man. My other instructors knew I answered every question quickly, but not quick enough for this man. He had slapped me with my favorite book, *The Adventures of Robin Hood*. Without finishing it, I returned the book to the teacher, conflicted about reading from the instrument of my torture.

The ill-mannered headmaster had a weakness — rum. His head held high, he strolled past local drunks sitting at the crossroad bar. He lifted a trap door on the counter and stepped back to Miss Mattie's secret chambers. None of the locals ever saw him tipping his glass, but Miss Mattie's boys let it slip that he drank his rum undiluted. His appetite for alcohol ran as fiercely as his fanatic beatings. He never staggered drunkenly or reeked of liquor when he left Miss Mattie's quarters.

People speculated about what else happened in her private quarters. Most folks thought it odd that Miss Mattie, the most powerful woman in the district, allowed the principal to torture her son Ricky. Strange events occur when the two most powerful people in the village convened. So many secrets and not a soul had the courage to cast the first stone and break the curse of silence.

Over time, I read the book, even as I equated the headmaster to the villains in Robin Hood's tales. I made my own bow and arrows and taught myself archery. My reputation as an archer spread. Ricky, Miss Mattie's son, asked me to make a bow for him. He gave me a shilling, enough money to buy lunch.

In the fourth grade, I saw more of Mr. Beastly's brutal personality. At the end of the day, he made us clasp our hands, close our eyes, and sing devotional hymns. He slung his leather strap across his back and prowled the school in search of anyone who dared to defy him. Written on the strap, in bold, were the letters S-C-O-R-P-I-O-N. Someone with an appetite for pain named that chunk of leather.

A finger gently touched my eyelids as I dutifully sang the evening hymn. I knew it was Gene, standing next to me. Bored as usual, he tried to get me involved in one of his pranks. Some instinct told me to open one eye and survey the scene before joining him. I saw the headmaster's legs in the shadows behind the blackboard. As he walked toward an opening he would bump into Gene and me fooling around. I froze, closed my eyes, and assumed my most pious posture. I sang, "Now the day is over, night is drawing nigh," as loud as I dared without faking piety.

Gene probably thought I "got in the spirits" when Mr. Beastly set upon him with leather. Wind swirled around me as Scorpion cut through the air and stung Gene's back. I cringed at every blow, yet I sang even louder to drown out the storm of slaps lashing the air. I would sing a thousand hymns to evade the sting in Scorpion's tail. I waited to feel the stings across my back. The blows never came.

After the singing, Gene left quickly and walked home alone as night drew near. Usually we strolled side by side, but I sensed he wanted to be alone. Perhaps I should have warned him, but I dreaded the beastly headmaster. Gene's family never sent him to church, and he got bored with the hymns we sang three times a day. Like Mamma, I loved to sing.

In this school, a warm-hearted boy who played little pranks with his cousin never found welcome. I could read and write very well, and I fit in. Gene preferred to work with his hands, and he felt the Scorpion strap across his back as he fought off boredom. After that, Gene retreated into his own world.

Chapter 28

As the sun shifted to the west, it cast long shadows on one side of the school. After drinking his lunchtime rum at Miss Mattie's shop, Mr. Beastly returned to unleash his favorite beating time. He marched the class to the shady side and shunted us in a circle. Scorpion belt in hand, he set up in the middle. Starting from on one end of the circle, he shot out questions as rapidly as lightning during an afternoon storm. If you failed to provide the answer he wanted, he lashed you with his Scorpion belt. He asked the girl on my right to complete a simile. She stumbled for words.

"You fool nuh," he chided the terrified child.

Scorpion's thick belt slapped the girl's back, and silent suffers, we stood motionless, lambs at the slaughter. If you knew an answer and tried to tell it to someone else, the headmaster pounced on you too.

He beat through half the circle, and then he reached Aubrey, the boy standing to my right. Aubrey stuttered a response. Mr. Beastly cut him short. I felt Scorpion's tail flicking through the air as it wailed across Aubrey's back.

"Rubbish, rubbish," the headmaster snarled.

Dust flew into the air every time he struck Aubrey. From the corner of my eye, I saw the expression on the headmaster's face. Amid this terror, his face overflowed with satisfaction.

"You skylarking man, skylarking nuh?"

He raised the Scorpion's tail and turned to me. I knew the answer to his simile. I waited. Our eyes locked.

"As mad as a hatter," I rasped, feeling the sweat mingling with the red dirt on my feet.

Mr. Beastly held Scorpion above me for an extra moment, and I looked into his soul, and he in mine. His dark pupils shined with the same glint I saw in the eyes of a rat that Father trapped.

Nightly, the rat harvested the first summer fruits from an orange tree behind our kitchen. The pest bit a hole in one of the oranges and moved to destroy other fruits without eating them. Father baited the rattrap and caught the beast. I saw fear in the rat's eyes as Father prepared to set the rodent on fire.

As a waning tempest depleted of energy, Mr. Beastly stopped beating for the day. He walked away from the circle, trailing Scorpion behind him. Ricky, standing next to me, shuffled his feet, and then stopped shaking. He would be next. He knew where to stand to avoid the licks from the teacher.

Ricky stuck by my side thinking that I would shield him from Mr. Beastly's fury. I felt awkward with the kind of influence he attributed to me. His family controlled all businesses in our neighborhood, and I was supposed to help him learn?

He often told lengthy narratives about the world of his family's cars and trucks. His family had an electric generator for their house, and occasionally he told me what he saw on TV. This offered me a glimpse of a new and intriguing realm of people with power. He disliked Gene, but I suspected Ricky wanted me to give him all my attention.

Ricky spread nasty stories about Gene to make my cousin seem an undesirable companion. Gene did not help his own cause; he despised school even as I grew to like it. In time, I outgrew my cousin's tales of raw head and bloody bones. Reluctantly, I let Ricky come between Gene and me.

Chapter 29

Razor-sharp gravel ripped my bare feet as I scurried home. The lame toe with its missing nail cried out a warning. I ignored the aches and bounced up the unpaved road. A throng of classmates filled the air with laughter. Their songs drifted through the gulley and echoed off the green hillside. The breeze carried a promise of an afternoon shower.

"Let me carry your book-bag, nuh? You stopped the headmaster from killing us with licks."

Sonny tried to take my bag. If you stopped the Scorpion, you became an unheralded hero for the day. I shook my head. The weight of the books under my arm comforted me. Books were my power.

Back at school, I enjoyed silencing the headmaster's rage, but I paid a price. I always needed to give the right answer, or he lashed me like any other child. I detested the man's whippings.

Voices thundered out of the bar as we approached the crossroad. The men were at it again, drinking Jamaican white rum and seething with the fury of an afternoon storm. I felt wary. At any moment, they might unleash a torrent of wrath-filled expletives on the child of a man they despised.

One of the drunks staggered through the half-open door. Rum, sweat, and the stench of fermenting limes oozed from him. He fixed his eyes on me and began a lucid sermon.

"The fathers have sinned, and the children are beaten down."

I paced nervously. Nobody knew about my father's sins. Abbot, the drunk, never set his foot in a church, but he evoked godly fear in my soul. I prayed that my classmates dismiss the speech as *rum talk* and not connect it to me.

With a dejected wail, Abbot cut short his sermon and lurched home. He did not get far. He propped himself on a bank of red soil by the road and wept. His head dropped to his chest as he called out to his long-deceased wife. A grown man never should cry so shamelessly.

His weeping echoed from the hollow hills, but nobody offered him comfort. Big men do not cry. Rum his remedy, he'd already drank his daily dose. Curious schoolchildren swarmed around him, seeking to quench their thirst for laughter.

Back at home, Father often scoffed at the drunk.

"Abbot's a no good rass, no good." Any man not in the sun tending his crops was good-for-nothing by my father's reckoning. Abbot topped his list of no good people.

When the downtrodden man lurched home, I saw an opportunity to show my loathing. I barked at him in my deepest monster growl. Halfway through the first growl he became stone-cold sober. In one quick move, he straightened up and blocked my path. The restless patter of the children's bare feet ceased. They broke into laughter, urging him on. A hand grabbed the back of my shirt and shoved me forward.

Abbot blasted more biblical wrath.

"Your father, Gilbert, sucks the sour grape and the children's teeth are set on edge."

His voice quivered with the credible emotion of a preacher. I tensed. Only folks who scorned Father called him Gilbert. The mention of the name meant that someone intended to poke fun at his failings. A tough man, Father fired back at anyone who teased him. Folks never taunted him to his face; instead, they directed their rage at my siblings and me.

Abbot spread his legs apart for balance and his sunken eyes washed me with contempt. He seemed poised to break the news that despite all pretentions, my family was also a *no good rass*. He got ready to reveal the family's darkest secret. Father, the best provider in the valley, had a sinister double that forced us to live on the edge at home.

"Gilbert, Gilbert sucks sour grapes," he mocked in his pious preacher's voice. Abbot glared with the fury of a dog after it killed a mongoose. I might be his kill.

This man had surely missed his calling. How could he know about our bitter life at home? Parson Brown was not in his league when it came to advocating guilt, shame, fire, and brimstone. His allusion to sour grapes passed on a heavy burden to me. Though I hardly knew what sour grapes meant, I hated the curse of my father's sins.

Abbot blew his sickly-sweet rum breath in my face. The odor reminded me of sterilizing alcohol and the sting of needles from my vaccinations. I recalled the stench of defeat from the funeral for Sonny's mother as the gravediggers drank rum to swallow their fear of death. I smelled fear: my own. No wonder the church faithful christened rum *devil-soup*.

I tried to shrink into the collar of my rough khaki uniform. My feet shuffled as I tried to blend into the crowd of other shoeless feet. In a swarm, they trapped me, pushing me back toward the blasphemous man.

"Heh-heh, Dan-Dan, you gwine get it." My fair-weather friends turned on me.

Abbot's eyes blinked, holding back tears, but for all his weeping, his eyes were barely moist. He gulped, and his huge Adam's apple bobbed. Unforgiving folks named the swollen organ a "rum ball," the trademark of an alcoholic.

A few drops of rain pelted the crowd. Abbot's shoulders slumped further, but mercifully, he stumbled on, cursing me as he left. The hills never forgave easily. They echoed every syllable, even repeating the plucking sound when he cried, "Suck."

Abbot never exposed my family's secret, and never relieved me of the yoke of concealing it. I assumed the role of the "goody-goody boy" to balance the life of my unhappy family.

The schoolchildren moved on. They were oblivious that a drunk just looked deep in my soul and saw the pain that I guarded so secretly. Trapped in a narrow valley with a pitiful future, I felt as useless as Abbot. I melted into the crowd.

I hated Abbot because he knew what I was hiding inside. He was free to drink because it freed him to grieve for his dead wife and vent his pent-up wrath on me. I had no such relief from my secrets.

By the time we climbed the hill and left the crossroad, my classmates seemed to have forgotten the drunk's scorn, but I could never again fit into their light, happy circle. Besides, the inspector had prophesied that I would *go far away* from this village.

Chapter 30

By the sixth grade, I adapted to the culture of fear that Mr. Beastly used to run his school. Hastily, I completed my assignments and avoided a beating. I sat in the front, sandwiched between Cal, the headmaster's nephew, and my new friend Ricky. Cal's big flashing smile and bright hazel eyes made him a favorite with the girls, but his charm never worked on his uncle.

Mr. Beastly beat Cal as no uncle should. Daily, I felt Cal shuddering next to me, in dire fear of this man. The headmaster beat the boy if his sentences were too short, if he added numbers incorrectly, or if he failed to meet the headmaster's cruel gaze. By some good grace, I finished my assignments and helped the boys next to me.

Cal always forgot to write the verbs in his sentences, so I edited his work. Many a day, Mr. Beastly nearly caught me fixing up his work. Outwardly, Cal bore his torment very well. When Mr. Beastly left the room, he lit up, but slumped in despair when the headmaster reappeared.

The only sign of rebellion Cal indulged was his over sharpened pencil. He always brandished its sharp point at arm's length as if trained at some invisible foe. Sometimes he poked himself with the pencil, as if priming his nerves for an imminent clash of wills.

His uncle had a secret, troubled past. Mr. Beastly had fathered a child with one woman and then married her sister. Our heads were almost touching as Cal whispered Mr. Beastly's secret to get even with his uncle, the tormentor. I kept the secret knowing that his uncle would surely beat him senseless if he revealed the family shame.

One day Mr. Beastly assigned bookwork to us and then left the school to attend to personal business. The atmosphere relaxed in the classroom. I turned around and chatted with Sonny and his friend Mikey.

When he first returned from the big city, Sonny performed better than the rest of us. He had attended superior schools in the city, but soon he struggled like most students. One of the boys whispered that Sonny's "near blood" heritage stunted his brain. They never let him forget his father, the incestuous Isaiah.

The butcher's daughter, Opal, started a delightful conversation. She made me laugh, and I loved watching her smile. For the first time, I noticed her pretty lips. Usually studious and quiet, Opal refused to pick up her pencil after Mr. Beastly left. Even though I tried to complete my assignment, I accomplished little because she kept telling tale after tale.

Mr. Beastly returned in a dark mood. He called me out first, as if he expected me to set the tone of the class.

"Show me y-o-u-r work," he snarled.

I shuffled papers and presented the few English assignments that I had completed. Without warning, his Scorpion strap flew out and stung my back repeatedly. I never felt such intense pain. It hurt all the way to my buttocks. I felt like my father sitting in the dark, on the wooden toilet seat, as the scorpion pierced his arse. I wanted to bawl, but I tried to be strong like Cal. He frequently endured this kind of torture without flinching.

I had no tolerance for pain and I almost pissed my pants. To withstand the stings, I numbed myself and retreated to a dark place far away from the misery. I refused to stay long in that dark place, though. Everyone seemed dazed.

Opal took her beating without a quiver. She seemed accustomed to pain, ignoring the wild flailing of a mad man. The headmaster only beat the two of us. Sonny and the rest of the students got off light that day.

As Mr. Beastly left the room, my classmates prayed to hasten their twelfth birthdays when they could transfer out of this primary school. Mikey spoke up first.

"I hate dat man. I can't wait to leave for Mocho Secondary School."

His hands snaked to his stomach to calm the torrents there.

"A don't care if I have to walk three miles to school, so long as I never see him again."

He pointed an angry finger at the headmaster's empty desk. His mother, an intern teacher at the school, failed to protect him from Mr. Beastly.

At the end of the day, I ambled home with Sonny and a band of boys through the crossroad. We passed Mr. Beastly's car parked alongside Miss Mattie's rum shop. He came to entertain his not-so-secret vices.

Beneath the verandah of the old shop, Maddah's gaunt figure stood like a bulletwood tree leaning sideways after a hurricane. A warner woman, her lamenting voice rang out across the square.

"Repent, repent. Sudden death and destruction upon the crossroad. Mmhmm, Mmhmm. B-l-o-o-d. I see a vision. B-l-o-o-d."

Maddah trudged for miles from the next village to warn people to atone their evil ways, or more blood would run at the crossroad. She braved the square and defied the people loitering there to deliver her warning.

From the rum bar, the stench of devil soup rum mingled with fermenting limes, mocked her piety. Afternoon shadows stretched off the battered zinc roof of the shop and covered the spot where the cutthroats had spilled Buffington's blood.

"Anything she says must happen. She have goat mouth." Sonny mumbled.

When goats feed on saplings, they strip away the bark and the plants wither and perish.

"Shhhh. Shet you mouth, Sonny. Me afraid of her."

Maddah's predictions always came true, though they were never about good times. She asked if anyone needed prayer, but folks fled her presence, with the drunk and foul-mouthed leading the way. Nobody wanted Maddah to set her "goat mouth" on them.

Her distant, weary eyes seem to wrestle with visions of death. I wondered if she had children my age. With the world on her shoulders, she looked a little like my mother after a night of battling her own visions.

"Walk good through the crossroad, children. Mmhmm, Mmhmm." She turned the traveler's blessing "walk good" into a foreshadowing of death.

She murmured once more, a deep grunt from such a frail figure.

"Mmhmm, Mmhmm."

As we tiptoed past her, she ceased her condemnation, excusing us from our father's sins. We wandered up the hill and the rum shop dropped out of view. Her voice cried out after us, ringing faintly off the hills.

"B-e-w-a-r-e, b-e-w-a-r-e, w-a-r-e!"

Chapter 31

The tension around Mr. Beastly and his students paled in comparison to the frantic atmosphere in our home. Most evenings we ate dinner in silence, unsure what might set my father off. When he fought with Mamma, he would spring to his feet and toss his dinner into the jaws of the waiting dogs. Flaring their teeth, they ceased being protectors of the family and became remorseless hounds of hell, snapping up every morsel. Later, they devoured my dinner too.

My family grew the most food in the valley, yet my siblings and I ate very little at dinner. We were almost as emaciated as Abbot, the village drunk. As I picked up the broken plates after the dogs licked them clean, I understood why Mamma ate silently and alone in the kitchen.

One of my earliest memories was the sound of clothes ripping, Father cursing, and Mamma crying as she fled his grasp. He followed her and flicked pieces of her torn yellow print dress on the ground. Mamma had made the dress with a Singer sewing machine that her grandmother bequeathed to her.

During my preteen years, I stayed ready to stop the next fight between my parents, but I could not prevent the clash. One evening, Mama sent me to the crossroad to buy bread. When I returned, Father sat at his favorite perch under the *good for nothing* mango tree.

He called me over and told me the disgusting details of the fight. He showed me how he punched my mother. He torqued his fist in the air.

Did he want me to take his side, or was he teaching me how to fight a woman? Neither appealed to me, and I ran to find Mamma.

She tried to wash the blood from her face. A gash above her eye where Father's fist landed dripped more blood. I failed to find the words to tell her how sorry I felt. If I only had been there, I might have stopped it.

My older sister Jan stayed a step away from where our parents fought. When I arrived, she still stood there, head bowed, pressing her uniform for school the next day. She never bothered to look up. I wanted to ask what had happened, but I could tell her mind went somewhere else far away from the tempest in our home.

Later, my other sister Hazel, a feisty spirit, told me she fought for Mamma. She rushed at my father, and he charged back. She ran for her life past the tank that held our precious drinking water. He threw a coconut-sized rock at her, and it smashed a hole in the roof of the tank. The rock remained stuck at the edge of the gaping hole in the roof, threatening to fall into our priceless drinking water. Nobody ever climbed on top of the tank to retrieve the rock. The rock lingered in the hole in the roof, as broken as our lives.

Next day, Mamma went to patch her face at the doctor. She threatened to report Father's abuse at the police station in town. The doctor mended Mamma's face but not her spirit. Silence replaced the beautiful hymns she sang for us at bedtime. I read books, so I let the stories take me away.

I waited for the police Land Rover to pull up below our house. They never came. People in my community often lacked the power to change their circumstances. We were spared the public shame of Father's arrest but keeping the family secrets came with a price. I would have preferred the unburdening resulting from telling others about our shame.

During a prior conflict, my father quelled his rage by taking his crowbar to Mamma's bedroom window. The following day he called me over to help him fix it. Another time, he took the door off the hinges. The next day we were putting them back on.

I resented the bitter task of cleaning up after his whirlwinds, but without complaining, I held the door while he reattached it to the doorjamb. In the calm after the storm, I cherished that fleeting peace. Mostly, I helped for Mamma's sake. She needed the privacy of her door back on its hinges. I quickly learned how to make a wooden dowel to plug holes in the doorpost. It suited my nature, fixing up broken things.

At home, my siblings and I never conspired to keep our troubles secret. Silent sufferers, we were too ashamed to tell anyone. We lacked the courage to seek relief in telling.

When I confronted Abbot at the square, he sounded as if he knew of the terror in our home and he was about to tell my classmates. His spouse, the village midwife, was my mother's confidante. Maybe she told him about Father's evil side.

I hoped Abbot might release me from the burden of keeping the family secret by telling the other children that my prominent family *was no good a rass,* no better than anyone in our narrow valley between the peaks. Instead, he unforgivingly tied my father's sin to me with his bold 'fathers have sinned' proclamation. Abbot did nothing to relieve my fear of becoming like my wife-beating father. For a man who knew so much, Abbot did pitifully little to change his or anyone's circumstances for the better.

Chapter 32

All day long, Mamma baked her black fruitcakes for our trip to visit her side of the family. For weeks, she soaked raisins in wine, and now she added them to her masterpiece. The smell of cinnamon and nutmeg drew my siblings and me to the kitchen. We took turns using the wooden spoon to mix eggs, butter, and aromatic spices in the *yabbah*, the mixing bowl. The *yabbah, a* giant ceramic basin fashioned from dark-red clay, was my favorite kitchen utensil.

We used a wooden spoon to crush brown sugar against the glazed sides of the *yabbah* and listened to the satisfying plop-plop as the batter became creamier and creamier. Mamma looked the other way we stopped stirring to poke a finger in the tempting mixture for a taste.

The next day, Mamma, my three siblings, and I left home for the trip. She needed a break from Father. He said he wanted to stay and care for the animals, but I knew he disliked Mamma's family.

We needed a ride to get down to the train station in the plains. Mamma's family lived across the valley on the other side of the mountain. It would be my first train ride.

As we waited by the piazza, a man on his way to town gave us a ride in a new, white Ford sedan. His dark complexion marked him as a man from out of our area. Most people in our village were a lighter mixture of European and African ancestry. This man's dark skin was common among the people on the savannah whose ancestors worked the sugar plantations for many generations.

An educated man, he came to our village and married a woman with the palest skin. Occasionally, a villager commented about his black skin. That never bothered him. He earned more money than all the locals put together. Hazel sat with him in the front. Her pale skin and red, curly hair striking a contrast to his dark color.

The man dropped us off where the railroad lines twisted across the plains. We boarded the train carrying the cakes and muffins that Mamma had made. Mamma trusted our fourteen-year-old sister, Hazel, to carry the bottle of homemade sorrel drinks up the steps. Sorrel is a special drink usually reserved for Christmas, but this was not an ordinary trip.

We were going back to the district where Mamma grew up to see our grandfather for the first time since my toddler days. Mamma also planned to meet up with her cousin who was visiting from the United States. She had not seen him for decades. We could hardly wait.

My younger brother and I should have sat apart on the train. Two years younger than me, he resented the assignment Mamma gave me to "tek care of the younger one." Out of our native element, we had very little territory to fight over, but we fought anyway. He challenged my authority, and I subdued him by crushing his fingers in my grip. We then settled down to watch the people around us.

Most of the passengers on the train were country folks dressed in their Sunday best, even though their best may have been ill-fitting shoes and mismatched clothes. A vendor came through the car selling sodas. He carried the drinks in a small metal bath pan packed with ice.

"Pepsi, ginger ale, orange, Kola Champagne, Teem," he called out.

The vendor shoved a Pepsi at a woman seated across from us.

"Pepsi's a birth control," she responded.

The man edged closer to her and whispered in her ear.

"No man can breed me," she bleated defensively.

They chuckled together, and since I failed to understand their references, I filed their words away until I grew old enough to understand. We drank our sorrel from the tiny, stemmed glasses that Mamma packed for the trip, and stayed away from the vendor's forbidden drink. Mamma took pieces of fried chicken from her handbag and passed them around.

The train wormed across the undulating foothills through patchy farmlands interrupting the flow of trees. We then climbed across hills similar to the limestone slopes where we grew up. Mamma told us to get ready for a ride through a tunnel cut in the mountain side. We darted from full sun to the pitch black of the tunnel and out again into daylight. She explained that the English built the railroads over a hundred years previously. The railroads connected the sugar plantations across the island. Many of the plantations closed, and trains lost ground to the convenience of automobiles.

Mamma kept one last surprise for us. She pointed out a house that Father owned when they first got married. The house, a two-story colonial structure, dwarfed our current home.

"Twelve bedrooms," she declared with pride as we sped past the house. They had even rented out one of the rooms to a tenant. Father sold the property and moved around until he returned to the family home. I wondered what turn in fortunes made him come back to our humble home in the hills.

Late in the afternoon, we finally we got off the train and walked to a house to meet our cousins from America. They turned out to be white folks. My cousin paid scant attention to my brother and me. His wife seemed to struggle to find kinship with us, a plain bunch of country folks. Her eyes watched us through an endless cloud of smoke flowing from a cigarette poised between delicate fingers.

We stayed with them for one night. The next morning, I itched for breakfast to be over, so we could walk up the mountains to Mamma's birthplace.

Chapter 33

My grandfather visited us back when I was a toddler, but I'd forgotten what he looked like. He looked like the white man on the oatmeal box in our kitchen. When he saw us, he darted back inside a darkened room, emerged with a small Bible, and read aloud. At eighty years old, he scanned the tiny prints without reading glasses. He read a story about a bad woman, implying my Mamma fit that role. I scorned him for that implication.

He declined to hug my mother, and she seemed uneasy in her childhood home. Strutting past her uncertain smile, he led us to the back of the house where a long ladder leaned against a guinep tree. He ambled up the ladder, picked some of the fruits, and handed them to us. This early in the season, the first fruits are always sour. We faked eating a few.

Mamma showed us the remains of the plantation house where she grew up. The house served as the residence of her ancestors when they held slaves. All that remained were limestone steps and a bleached foundation. Duck ants had eaten the woodwork to the ground.

She often told us about growing up in this old house filled with memories of her ancestors. Her only brother still kept an original record of someone in our family selling slaves. Mamma's stories always seemed unreal, distant. Now standing on the foundation of the plantation house, I made an uneasy connection to the fact that a mere four generations ago, my foreparents had been white slaveholders.

After slavery ended, our relatives swapped off their land for whatever supplies they needed. My family inherited light skin like white people but never the money to back up that status. I could not live up to the expectation of having money and power like white folks.

On her maternal side, Mamma descended from the Maroons, a group of runaway slaves who mingled their bloodline with the indigenous Taino people. The Maroons fought a guerilla war with the English and eventually won some freedom.

My maternal grandmother died when Mamma was a toddler. Mamma grew up with her father's family in the ruins of the Great House. She was the darkest person in the household. I never met anyone from the Maroon side of her family.

With the ghosts of my ancestors at rest beneath the weeds, we returned to the smaller house where my grandfather lived. If ever there were a true reflection of a witch, it would be my grandfather's new wife. She depicted all the attributes of her storybook alter ego, except for the lack of a black hat. An unusually long, thin nose reached toward her chin. A web of wrinkles twisted across her thin face. The eternal optimist, Mamma greeted her warmly.

"Mawning, Miss Liza."

Miss Liza barely replied. She puffed on a hand-rolled cigarette with the lit end turned inside her mouth, and the butt jutting sideways from her lips. Few ever mastered that skill, and even fewer attempted to speak while thus occupied.

"See my oldest daughter. Her middle name is Liza, just like you." Mamma pointed at Hazel. Miss Liza removed the cigarette and looked mildly interested.

"Come 'ere, make me see you."

"Uh-uh," she declared to Mamma. "She is goin' to have bad luck just like me."

"Just like me," she repeated as she spat the cigarette to the ground.

That ended Mamma's attempt to have a light conversation with the woman. A lost look clouded Hazel's face. She loved her name.

In my mind, I started a dialogue with the witch. *You do not appear to be someone with bad luck. You have defrauded my grandfather of acres of the family land. You ran off with other men numerous times, but my grandfather always took you back. You have nothing in common with my sister Hazel.*

Jan, the other sister, escaped all the attention. Two years younger than Hazel, she often deferred to her older sister. Jan mastered the art of vanishing when things got uncomfortable.

We left the remains of the plantation clinging to the hillside and escaped the witch and her bad luck. My grandfather, the last of the white men to live on the plantation, slipped back into the shadows inside his house.

Mamma's mood lifted as she led us away. Tales of her childhood amidst these hills came to life as we climbed. Every tree told a story. My father's impatient voice was not here to prod her to trot at his hurried pace.

The path ended in a tiny level encircled by soft blue peaks. If there were any ghosts in this minuscule plain, they were as light and pleasant as the cool breeze touching us with a complete absence of sound. In the middle of the plain, Aunt G waited for us by her small house. My grandmother had died when Mamma turned two; Aunt G filled in, helping to bring up my mother.

A field of sweet potatoes surrounded Aunt G's house. From their purple blooms, I knew they were ready for harvesting. Folks whose names I knew from Mother's tales of her childhood drifted through the purple blooms to squeeze our hands and poke us with warm curiosity. Mamma often told us of these cousins as we sat in our kitchen back home. Now they were old men, schooled in the art of storytelling and drinking Aunt G's coffee.

Night fell softly as a cool sheet let fly over a sleepy child. With his "early to bed, early to rise" doctrine, my father would have long ago driven off the guests. Mamma let us stay up late listening until the men grew tired and walked away, shadows into the night.

"They can't sleep in the dark," Mamma told Aunt G as we got ready for bed. The kerosene lamp in the room spluttered and struggled to stay alight. Mamma pointed out the jagged hole in the delicate lampshade. Heeding her concern, Aunt G stuck a piece of paper over the hole and dimmed the light.

Mamma tucked us in cautiously, eyeing the makeshift shade. I knew the lampshade alarmed her. She always sensed impending danger. Reluctantly, she left to share the room next door with Aunt G. I fell into a deep sleep and drifted into a lucid dream.

In my dream, there is fire all around me. Long fingers of crackling, yellow flames leap at my face. Heat sears my head. I sense the presence of an adult couple bustling around me, shielding me from the flames, and vocalizing their concern.

"See the little pickney dem though, eh."

The bed shakes violently as if someone is trying to prod me awake.

"Fire, fire," I heard myself shout.

I spring out of bed and shake my younger brother awake. We scream and run to find Mamma in the next room.

The women rushed in, gasping at the flames climbing angrily up the curtains beside the bed. Mamma froze and pointed to the lamp with its top blown to bits.

Aunt G grabbed the two-gallon enamel mug of water that everyone kept indoors and tossed a stream at the flames. I ran with her to the tank to get more water to battle the fire. Soon the flames died down.

We sat in the kitchen, talking to calm our nerves. I languished in a corner, hugging my knees to stop them shaking. Aunt G picked up a broom and began to sweep the kitchen floor until she calmed down.

Mamma made mint tea.

"Midwife said you born with a caul."

"A caul?"

"An extra flap of skin over your eyes. You have a gift.

"W-h-a-a-t?"

"You see things other people can't see."

Mamma said my quick alarm saved my brother's life. Unusual people claim special gifts. I never wanted to be unusual, so I took no credit, nor did I tell her about my vision of the people who shielded me from the flames.

The fire broke the enchantment of the valley, and two days later, we took the wobbly train back to our side of the mountain. We boarded a blue minivan with a rusty BMC emblem on the front. Halfway up the hill, the driver stopped to pour water into the radiator. Steam shot into the passenger compartment, and I ran for the door.

"Sit down bwoy," the driver snarled.

Mamma spoke up calmly.

"No! Sir, for what he's been through, that's expected." In formal English, she told him how I saved my brother from the fire.

Mamma's command of standard English was much better than I imagined. She barely finished elementary school and usually spoke a mixture of the local Patois.

The driver kept staring into the steamy vent of the radiator. Tiny beads of sweat dotted his nose, but he said nothing. A mother spoke up for her son, and he knew to leave that alone. He took us miles out of his way to the village square.

Chapter 34

A charismatic evangelist came to the Saturday Church by the crossroad and began a revival campaign to save souls from hell. Even though we never attended Saturday church, we dropped in to check out the revival event.

At the revival, Mass Harry, the versatile sawyer man who cut our cedar trees, played his guitar and led the congregation in songs. Eyes closed, he plucked on the guitar strings as his lips mouthed every note. I had never heard a song that offered more promise than the one they were singing.

"Jesus gave water from a well that could not run dry."

A promise of water from a source that would not run out drew people in. In our limestone hills, we often suffered from harsh droughts when crops withered, and animals hobbled about on scrawny legs. Only if you owned a deep tank with water from the rainy season did you have enough water to boil yams for dinner.

The people in the church continued to sing about a woman who drank from the abundant well.

> And she went away singing,
> And she came back bringing,
> Others saw the water
> That was not in the well.

I caught the image of women lining up to get some of this precious liquid. The preacher stepped to the pulpit and offered more of this "living water." He pointed straight at my heart and challenged,

"Oh, taste and see ..."

This was the most convincing preacher to set foot in our mountains. Some of the foulest of the foul-mouthed citizenry forsook their ways and came to follow the teaching of this man.

Mass Harry's beautiful teenage daughter, Miriam, sang in the choir. A young man, Tempest, watched from the shadows outside the church. He was courting Miriam, and he never let her out of his sight.

Most people disapproved of his courtship because he was a charmless, moody man. Moreover, Tempest had never joined any church, and even the charismatic evangelist failed to win his soul. Scripture forbade Christians "becoming unequally yoked" with nonbelievers, but he still stalked her.

If he chose to, Tempest could brag about his farming skills. He worked tirelessly, and bountiful crops of yellow yams rewarded his toil. Father hired him to plant yams during the growing season. Tempest got no special breaks because he was a distant cousin; Father only hired workers who matched his passion for hard work.

We were always on good terms with Mass Harry, and he invited Mamma to the revival services. Gradually, she became a follower of the charismatic preacher. She was never an ungodly woman, but duties in the kitchen kept her chained to the fireside. She never found the time for formal worship. Usually, her devotion consisted of prayers and singing hymns prior to bedtime.

While Mama's action intrigued me, I was awestruck when Father joined her in church and the preacher scheduled their public baptism. Everyone in our household, including the dogs, came out to witness the ceremony. Father survived the immersion in the baptismal pool, but, to my disappointment, no white doves descended from heaven to celebrate. As he began to attend Saturday services, I thought he might find his mellow side and walk a little slower.

He changed very little. His favorite Bible story was still about the man who prayed alone in his closet instead of in a public place. Without ceremony, Father continued to send us with some of the fruits of his farm to a widow at the other end of our village.

I wondered how long Father could follow the church dogma to keep the Sabbath holy. The doctrine of no work from sundown Friday to sundown Saturday clashed with our lifestyle. Father would never ignore his animals in the fields, or the Saturday task of chopping wood for the kitchen fire. Still, he looked very elegant in a suit as he got dressed for church.

My two older sisters got off easily. Hazel and Jan were established in the Sunday church that we normally attended, and they stayed there. My brother and I accompanied our parents to service on Saturdays, but we always took care of the animals on our homestead on the Sabbath. We were never true Sabbath keepers.

Shaggy, our dog that replaced Rally followed us to church one night. He waited quietly outside the church door, but Bell, the neighbor's noisy dog, challenged him to a fight. Their snarling and barking disturbed the ceremonies, and Deacon York, one of the leaders, went to break up the fight.

He tossed Bell down the precipitous slope behind the church. The dog crashed onto the rocks below. Father grasped my hand and my brother's in a single paw and pranced toward the deacon. His other hand held the cap that soon would grace his bald dome. Father moved quickly to rescue Shaggy before Deacon York tossed him too. In the dim light outside the church, Father shoved his face into the deacon's and growled.

"York," he threatened. "If it was my dog you throw over there, blood would'a run out here tonight, man. Blood man."

York, though decades younger, retreated from the shock of Father's threating posture. Father did not have a pocketknife to *run blood*, but his dogs were his family, and he always spoke up for his family.

"Come," he ordered.

We stepped into the night feeling the cool air sliding off the nearby peak. Little fingers of light from the church windows poked at us retreating into the dark. We passed Tempest, merged in the gloom, and pining after Miriam.

Father stopped going to church, and our obligation to attend with Mamma ceased. My brother Serge and I went back to Sunday services, and they accepted us, forgetting we left to worship with the "other" church.

It took the dog, Bell, a long time to recover from his mishap. After that, he stopped barking and snarling like a beast.

Mamma continued to attend Saturday church despite Father's ill-tempered objections. With her quiet demeanor and her beautiful soprano voice, she won the affection of the congregation. My father at no time wanted to share her with anybody, but she did not quit despite his antagonism.

Mass Harry's church organized a concert, and Mamma decided to sing a duet with Uncle Mack. She planned to sing in English while Uncle sang the counterpart in Spanish. From her nightly singing at bedtime, we were confident that Mamma would perform very well. We eagerly anticipated her performance.

At the last minute, the woman who coordinated the church program took Mamma's place and sang with Uncle Mack. The woman, a teacher, yielded more influence than my humble mother. The teacher always saw Mamma as an upstart rival in the church.

That exceeded Mamma's tolerance. She refused to attend the concert. Uncle Mack sang with the teacher and won great acclaim from the congregation. Mamma stopped going to church.

One day, a pack of deacons came to our house to woo my parents back to church. They strutted up to our doorsteps with Mass Harry in the lead. Father greeted them with his Swivel Jack, a long flexible rod used in the old days for fighting. When swung, the rod coiled around the victim's body, causing stinging pain. Virtually unbreakable, the staff could deliver blow after blow. Unlike the killing power in a machete, the Swivel Jack was a shock weapon, intending to belittle the opponent's fighting skills. Father delighted in catching his adversary off guard.

Fortunately, one of the men grabbed my father's arm before he could strike Mass Harry. He displayed another skill: light on his feet, he sprinted off our property. With a heavy heart, I watched him flee. Our lives had crossed many times before during more pleasant times.

Chapter 35

Another murder in the crossroad fulfilled Maddah's bloody prediction. Our little community of Brickman soon earned the name Kill-Man. Boys who came to our school from the other districts teased us about the two killings in rapid succession. They labeled us "cutthroats" and hovered in threatening groups.

Sonny and I banded together for support as we walked through the square to buy lunch. Like any other country boy, Sonny no longer wore shoes. He probed the paint marks on the asphalt with his toes as I told the other children how it happened.

One morning, soon after Buffington's bloodstains grew faint at the crossroad, Father's urgent voice woke us up. He tried to tell my mother some frantic news, but he struggled to get the words out.

"Temp, Tempter, Tempest killed Mass John last night at the crossroad," he blurted.

He tried to say that the previous night while we slept, Tempest cut the throat of Mass John, the local carpenter. Mass John was a reputable tradesman with a wife and three children. The trouble started when Tempest had an affair with Mass Harry's daughter, Miriam. She became pregnant, and the faithful read her out of the church. She moved in with Tempest.

After the birth of the baby, Miriam fought with Tempest, and she fled to Mass John's arms. Perhaps she thought that his status as the best carpenter in the area might shield her from the menacing Tempest. Astonishingly, Mass John deserted his family and moved in with Miriam. No one expected him to forsake his elegant wife for the younger Miriam.

They walked through the village, hugging tighter than two planks nailed to the kitchen wall, but an uneasy air surrounded her. She studied every face trying to glean news of Tempest's next move.

She had reason to be wary. Tempest boldly proclaimed that he intended to bring bodily harm to anyone who put hands on his woman.

During the Christmas season, Tempest could no longer bear to see Miriam with Mass John. After the festivities were over and the people went home, he lay in wait at the crossroad. Everyone must pass through the crossroad.

Our family ceased to participate in the Christmas merriment since the shooting star dropped an omen over the square. We were already in bed as Tempest waited in the darkness at the crossroad.

Tempest left his weapon, the honed down blade of a farmer's most valuable tool, his machete, next to the bloodstains. All the time Miriam continued with Mass John, Tempest stewed and sharpened the long blade of his machete until it became a stiletto-thin killing tool.

When we returned to school in January, the paint marks on the ground told the story. A few circles marked where Mass John spilled his first drops of blood next to the giant ackee tree. He dripped small circles as he ran, and a large circle marked where he crumbled to a heap in the center of the crossroad.

I wondered how Mass John ran that far. He was a middle-aged man, slow on his feet. Tempest, on the other hand, moved like lightning. Not a single person knew how Miriam escaped Tempest's wrath. Next day, she fled the village with nothing but the clothes on her back. Her father, Mass Harry, continued his role as the lead deacon for the church, and salvaged his family's dignity.

Chapter 36

My schoolmates moved from the dusty wooden floors of the old church-school to a newly built elementary school. The last public ceremony held in the old church-school was my Uncle Mack's funeral. On the day of the funeral, Mr. Beastly dismissed school early, so his staff and students could attend the services.

The headmaster made a shocking tribute to a man who held no public office. Mr. Beastly never dismissed school early for any one, but Uncle Mack knew how to reach peoples' hearts.

Uncle's health declined when he began smoking cigars with a group of neighbors. Father grew furious. Even though Father smoked hand-rolled cigarettes, he held Uncle to a higher standard. Moreover, one of Uncle Mack's smoking partners held low esteem in the village.

This man let his wife do all the hard work on the farm while he sat resting in the shade. He never sharpened his machete, a sign of a lazy man. After his wife labored all day in the field, she came home and cooked dinner. Her husband sat like a sentinel, watching as she cooked.

On our way home from school, we saw him staring earnestly at her through the open door. His zeal earned him the nickname Kitchen-Fire, the man who idled by the kitchen. Not even his nickname made him budge from his perch. Kitchen-Fire made my father's list of undesirable people even before the man gave Uncle Mack his first cigar.

Uncle started to get frequent colds and had trouble breathing when he performed strenuous activities. One morning Father called us to Uncle's bedside. Uncle Mack wheezed and panted, and I knew that, like Cousin Cedric, he was getting ready for that long journey. Father shoved his box of Shag tobacco at Salaman, the neighbor who always carried a newspaper. The man grasped it greedily, seeking to fill his immense appetite for alms from the dead and dying. Father never rolled another cigar.

Uncle Mack passed on quietly in his sleep. In the morning, Father went to the cellar and retrieved the boards that Mass Harry hewed from our cedar tree many years earlier. The local carpenter and his team came and carried off the planks.

Later, we went to the carpenter's house to see what they were making with the boards. The carpenters sawed and planed the wood to reveal its fresh, cinnamon-red hue. They made a coffin. This was the finest piece of cabinetry ever made, a fitting tribute for a man who came home to his family. So, this was why Father guarded the boards so carefully all these years, keeping secret their somber purpose.

Before the funeral, I went to pick up my pants from Jacob the tailor at the crossroad. He had diligently remade a pair of black cotton trousers that another uncle sent from Canada. Jacob's hard work barely showed. The garment looked slightly used and oversized.

As I waited for Jacob to finish ironing the pants, I recalled his chronicled life. The tailor had tried his hand at palm reading. When we were younger, my friends all lined up at his shop to have our palms read. My neighbor Wesley, the bravest, went first.

"You, you will live so long that they have to sun your collar-collarbones."

Jacob's slight stutter gave an air of credibility to his prediction. His forecast meant that Wesley would live so long that his flesh would waste away from his collarbones. Wesley's great grandchildren would need to carry him into sunlight to prevent his collarbones from getting dank and moldy. Ol' folks considered it an honor to live that long.

I plucked up the courage and offered my palm. He found a lot to read in the few lines on my palm. As usual, he took his time. I dismissed his forecast that my parents might try to harm me. How could they? They only lived for their children.

"By the time you are in your middle years, you will have great wealth," he prophesied as he grasped my fingers and flipped my hand upward.

"Middle age?" I asked.

He squinted at my hand.

"When you are about forty-five years old."

Who could wait that long for good fortune to call? I will go far in life, so said the inspector. I pulled my hand away. Jacob talked too.

He moved from child to child, giving each a prediction of long life. We latched on to Jacob's every word. Children expect to outlive their elders. Their smiles held rich promises for tomorrow.

Back in his other role as a tailor, Jacob showed me how to carry the black pants to keep the seams that he pressed with his special iron. I walked home and dressed for the funeral.

My dad skipped the church service. He organized the digging of the grave and other formalities for burial. He left before we got to the gravesite. He never witnessed the final rite of his favorite brother. Men in my village avoided funerals and the shame of crying in public.

I was the only one crying at Uncle Mack's funeral. I missed the irrepressible laughter of the ol' man and the feel of his light touch on my shoulder. I missed him calling me Buck, and his poor attempt to re-create the yellow rice from his days in Cuba. I will never again hear the string of Spanish expletives that meant nothing to us other than that he had trouble remembering the local Patois.

"Who shit there?"

No longer would I hear him calling out in feigned impropriety when he meant to bring levity to the untimely release of gas from a child's untrained bowels. He could soften any blow with his laugh, and the hills rang gently while laughing back at him. Now our valley must resume echoing Father's toil instead of my uncle's mirth.

Someone placed a hand on my shoulder. I looked up to see a woman who taught me in the junior classes at the elementary school. She held me, giving me permission to cry. I shoved my hands into the pocket of the ill-fitting pants and let the freedom of my tears wash over me.

Chapter 37

Mr. Beastly, the headmaster, continued to whip his students into submission in his new school. I dreaded telling my father about the lashes that I received. He might show up to school in the silence right after morning devotions, when we least expected. I pictured Father approaching with his machete cradled in his arm. He may well thrust his head close to the headmaster, rebuke the man, and set the air alight with his favorite cuss words.

My classmates would exaggerate my father's words to taunt me for the rest of my life. Nothing was worth the ridicule. It is unlikely that my father could have changed how the principal ran his school.

These were dark, brutal days when things stayed unchanged like an old mountain. A silent sufferer, I chose not to complain, and instead endured the intimidation of Mr. Beastly's Scorpion belt.

Mr. Beastly only relaxed on Thursday afternoons when the girls tried their hand at needlework and the boys were supposed to work on a craft. We never *crafted* anything. Instead, we spent the afternoon pumping water from an underground reservoir up to a tank about twenty feet high. The water then ran down through pipes to Mr. Beastly's house to supply his indoor plumbing needs.

Mr. Beastly put Cal in charge of the boys pumping water and went to do his chores. Cal stood at his finest during these times. He barked orders at the boys just like the headmaster. Eager to get out of the classroom, the boys stormed the pump and fought for a position on the line. Each tried to win the honor of being the last person on the pump as the aerial tank overflowed.

I kept back from the press of boys in line. My father sent me to get an education, certainly not to pump water for Mr. Beastly. He would have to use a pit-toilet if he relied on me to pump water for him.

Just before the tank overflowed, Cal shooed the boys away and beckoned Ricky and me to the pump. After a few strokes the aerial tank overflowed, and we proclaimed that we had done all the grunt work.

The boys let out a sarcastic cheer and sprinted away. They trampled Mr. Beastly's flower garden in a mad dash to get back to the classroom. Their whooping and yelling might earn them a whipping from the humorless principal, but nobody cared. We filled up the principal's tank and it overflowed into his yard. We granted him a favor, and he could flush his toilet.

A kind teacher, Mr. Sanderson, thought of a better way for the boys to use their time. He organized an academic quiz game on these Thursday afternoons. Soon he turned it over to me because I could quickly make up questions based on the books I read. Mr. Sanderson watched quietly. His smile overflowed his face and radiated over the group. When school dismissed, he gave me a shiny coin and numerous compliments.

Once we got to the shops at the crossroad, I bought *bullas* (giant cookies) and cheese. I shared my bounty with Sonny, my younger brother Serge, and a small pack of other boys. We ate hungrily after a long day at school. I further cemented my role as the unwilling leader of this band of boys.

Chapter 38

Before he passed away, Uncle Mack signed a secret deal to sell his forty acres to the American bauxite mining company. They paid him in dribbles. As the money trickled in, he promptly wasted it on women. After his death, an agent from the company brought a check to my aunt who lived in Uncle Mack's house. Father chased the agent away.

Salaman, our neighbor, hurried to the scene. On matters of estate and trust, he was "head cook and bottle washer." He called out, folded his newspaper, and scampered after the agent. Salaman placed an arm around the agent's shoulder and led him away. Puzzled, I watched. Men never embraced each other like that. He quickly gained the agent's confidence. I read his lips.

"Gimme the check, man. I will give it to them."

He stretched out his hand, imploring. The agent handed over the envelope, and Salaman grasped the packet and slipped it in his newspaper. Father focused on venting his fury at the bauxite company and missed Salaman's treachery. He trusted Salaman, his cousin and dear friend. Salaman wrote my father's own last will and testament. Aunt Edith never saw a penny of the money.

The mining company also bought up Cousin Pa Sam's rich farmland. They paid him a few pitiful dollars and moved his family to a scrap of land near the main road. In his new home, there were no coffee trees or a trail for Pa Sam's horse to canter.

Bushes and vines quickly overgrew the trails where his son, Gene, and I used to roam. Moments with my dear cousin were gone forever.

Educated men from the towns worked the land deals. "Eminent domain," they claimed. The government owned the right to take property and dispose of it as they saw fit. Illiterate neighbors swapped their land for small amounts of cash. An aging man across from the valley below my home signed his "X" and turned over acres for the cash equivalent of a few meals.

The island just converted from the English currency to the new Jamaican monetary system, and the value of money confused folks. The government sold out the people again.

Most people felt that the bauxite company at no time would mine their land. Since World War II, they'd threatened to dig up the soil beneath our homes and never carried out the threat. My father disagreed. When he traveled, he saw the bauxite mines in other parts of the country. He understood the need for raw materials from his experience working in the giant munition's factories during World War II. Father pushed his older children to leave the mountains before they were finished with school.

Chapter 39

Ma Ann, Gene's mom, stopped visiting our house to buy produce for the market. A Rasta man showed up in her place. He adored Mamma's home-baked pastries, her freshly brewed coffee, and her patient manner. The time they spent talking was worth more than the price of the produce he collected.

As the man approached, he whistled a gospel song that the Rastafarians modified to suit their faith. The wind carried the tune.

"Someday, someday, I'll go where Jah lives."

Rastafarians adapted their teachings from the Bible. They named their God *Jah*, shortened from Jehovah, the Judeo-Christian deity. Rasta celebrated their Pan African roots, recognizing the Ethiopian emperor, Selassie, as divine.

The roots of our visitor slightly favored his European side over his African ancestry. The piercing blue eyes and light complexion marked his European heritage. However, he found identity with black people. Europeans never claimed lineage among curly haired, light-skinned natives who were born to unwed black mothers. Africans left back on the continent never reached out either.

The whistling got louder. Then I saw the red milk crate on his shoulder. His white hair fell sideways off his head as if he carried a cross rather than the crate. A thick, graying beard tapered to a point on his chin. After each step, his eyes came alive, burning with the resolve of a kerosene lamp on a moonless night.

He limped a little, a light step, then a hop. His undulating gait made him walk as if he were pinned to the rhythm of a distant reggae beat. Sometimes the tempo rang crisp and clear, and he stepped boldly. Other times the beat grew fainter in the wind, and his step faltered.

Whatever grace he lost in his step, he made up for with his hopping style. He was an ol' man, but Mamma taught us to see people as relatives: Uncle, Auntie, Nana, or Tata.

Mamma caught the tune on the winds. Her smile twinkled all over her face.

"Braman a come."

As the first Rastafarian in our district, Braman was a curiosity. His name meant brother man of the Rastafarian faith. My father only called him by his Christian name, Zachariah. No one else did. He was our cousin, and Father knew him long before he became a "brother man." Furthermore, the Rasta brethren, with their appetite for smoking ganja, failed to make Father's short list of favorite people.

Braman did not smoke ganja. Older men in our community never smoked the weed. He greeted Mamma with a grimace of a smile through the bush of his beard.

"Auntie," he exclaimed with the true joy of a child. People called my mother "Auntie" out of respect for the fact that she married my father, Uncle Gil.

Mamma enjoyed his company, but he ignored me. I knew to sidestep this bearded Rasta man. Long ago, we had our war and made our peace at the crossroad.

We quarreled during my first few years of elementary school as I walked with my classmates past his house to buy lunch from Miss Mattie's shop at the square. Braman postured in his verandah and boasted that he could lay an egg like a chicken. The children clapped and cheered him on.

Behind Braman, the proud Lion of Judah, the Rasta man's standard, hung limply on a flag stuck to the wall. Next to the lion, a framed photograph of Emperor Haile Selassie smiled at us. Braman and the Emperor could pass for twin brothers except for the Emperor's pith helmet. The hat swallowed his head and half his ears.

Braman flaunted an egg up high for all to see. Clean and white, it looked freshly laid. He cleared his throat, unclasped his belt, and dropped his trousers.

"Now, ah, I gwine lay another one." He smiled at his captive audience, and I knew from the twinkle in his eyes that he meant every word.

His belt buckle clanged to the floor as he turned his backsides to the crowd exposing his underpants. He slipped his fingers behind the waist of his underpants, getting ready to drop them next to his trousers. He groaned as if bearing down to push out an egg. A frantic girl pointed and screamed.

"He's he goin' to show his batty, heh, heh."

Bodies swept past to take a closer look. Embarrassed that my cousin intended to drop his underpants and expose his batty for the world to see, I sought to save the face of the family. I knew where eggs came from.

"Braman," I jeered in my best Patois, "your mouth favor de fowl's batty."

He straightened up with a fierce flickering of his hawk eyes and grunting indignantly. For an instant, he became the Rasta man's ferocious Lion of Judah, getting ready to strike me dead for comparing his mouth to a chicken's buttocks.

Keen to join the unfolding drama, the children broke out in one of the many local taunts.

> Rain a fall
> Breeze a blow
> Chicken batty out de door

Even tots knew a jingle that could make you feel like your backside lay exposed to the wind and rain.

Sensing that he lost the moment, Braman pulled up his pants and fastened his belt. One hand reached up and tugged his beard defiantly. He glared at me.

"A gwine to tell Auntie," he threatened and ambled away.

No, I thought. Auntie, my Mamma, schooled us to respect the ol' folks. Moreover, she already had a hard time raising four children and dealing with the constant tension with Father. Why should I bring home more problems? I loved Mamma too much to cause her further anguish, so I sulked behind Braman as he hobbled to Miss Mattie's store.

Most boys my age tormented hapless people and got away with it. I could not. Only a few feet from this same spot, Abbot had cursed me with my father's sins because I growled at him.

Out of earshot of the other children, I begged quietly in my best quivering church voice.

"Braman, could you forgive me —" and the rest stuck in my throat.

He hauled himself upright and looked me over with a bit of wonder in his eyes. Clearly, he never expected me to seek him out and apologize.

I waited for his answer. Miss Mattie's machete thudded as she chopped salted codfish into little chunks for her customers. I counted the slow thuds as the blade hacked into the hardwood cutting block. Pickled mackerel marinating in brine-filled barrels behind the counter flooded the air with a thick, nauseating odor. Outside the door, the midday sun paused, marking the uncertainty. Braman grumbled before speaking.

"Awright then, a won't tell Auntie."

He gave his graying beard an extra stroke, and his eyes descended to mine as if his decision came from a higher power. Thankfully, he spoke quietly. Under no circumstances would I want my classmates to hear that I begged for forgiveness from this often-ridiculed ol' man.

"Sing praises," he muttered and hobbled away. Braman was always a contented man.

I slipped into the crowd and headed back to school. Mamma never once mentioned anything about a fowl's batty. He kept his promise and never told her. He also stopped laying eggs for schoolchildren.

Chapter 40

On Thursdays, Braman came to pick the squash we called "cho-cho," and collect bundles of peppermint for the market. Mamma grew the produce in a plot behind the house. Sometimes Braman harvested limes from the trees around our property. Father rarely sold him any oranges. These he kept for the other peddlers who bought in bulk and probably paid a better price.

Mamma gave Braman coffee and some of her freshly baked coconut cake. His beard seemed to get in the way, trapping crumbs from the pastry. Nobody minded. He made the strangest grunting noise, clearing his throat as he ate happily. You might think that he was in pain until you saw the twinkle of delight in his eyes. He always grunted as he prepared to say something witty.

Folks told a tale of Braman's experiences with the Rastafarian brethren. In his youth, he left the seclusion of our mountain village and joined the brethren in the plains. During one of their ceremonies, they tied him up and prepared to offer him as a sacrifice. He broke free before they knifed him. He mounted on his donkey and fled back to the safety of our district. Nobody ever asked him to confirm this story. The brethren were not known to participate in human sacrifice, but tales persisted beyond any evidence of truth.

Years later, the donkey died and Braman became his own beast of burden. He won a place among local storytellers who tailored his image to fit any role they assigned him. Not a soul knew how he secretly felt about being despised as the ragged Rasta man, the hapless clown, or the man who tried to lay chicken eggs for children.

Mamma and Braman often talked about religion. His interpretation of the Bible had enough twists to get him banished from any church. Backing up his version of the Bible with animated gestures, he added more life to the stories than my Sunday school teacher. He took a deep breath, and his meager chest heaved upward. He puffed into the air and grunted.

"See God there."

He pointed to the invisible trail of air exhaled from his bearded face. Braman looked around for a challenge, but no one thought much of his defiance to religious doctrine. The churches depicted God as a white man with a great, long, flowing beard. The breath of God never came from the chest of an old, despised man.

Mamma, however, looked past his appearance to see his dignity. She seemed to sense the secret pain of this Rasta man whose limp overtook the limber youth of foregone years. Mamma saw his need for acceptance and treated him as if he were an aging parent.

Father neither embraced nor objected to the bearded man. Occasionally, he joined the discussion between Braman and Mamma. As the debate heated up, Father shortened the visit.

"Zachariah, you talk too much, man."

Braman bristled at the mention of his Christian name. No longer a Rasta man, he assumed his mortal role of collecting produce for the market.

"Uncle Gil, me gone," he mumbled and then hobbled toward me.

For all the years that he came to our house, he never called me by name. Perhaps he never knew my name. Instead, he gave a special grunt or a merry twinkle in his eyes as he motioned for my help. His beard, thick as plumage on a chicken's batty, hid the smile that lit his eyes.

"Auntie, me gone," he sang, and then he signaled that he needed my assistance.

Without comment, I helped him pick up the crate of produce. I knew my place in this adult world where children were silent "little people."

His wiry body possessed more strength than his frame implied. Many a time as I helped him raise the milk crate, it felt heavy enough for two men. He stumbled under the weight and meandered away. He left whistling the same tune that we heard as he approached.

"Someday, someday, I'll go ..."

Chapter 41

One Saturday, Father and I walked to the other side of the village to buy a calf from a woman. On our way, we passed the crossroad. A few loafers gathered at the rum bar drinking the foul-smelling, over proof rum from thick tumblers.

As a younger boy, I would take a beating rather than pass by the rum bar on a Saturday. As I grew older, I tolerated the smell and the brooding mood of the men drinking white rum. After the two murders at the crossroad, many of the faithful drunks stopped going to the square. The square became quieter, and the gloom surrounding the rum bar lifted.

A few idlers remained to ridicule anyone who seemed different, or anyone who avoided the tranquil shadow of their drink. My father was definitely different, and he often became their favorite target.

As Father and I passed, one of the drunks, Money-Roy, shuffled over with a mocking smile. Money-Roy and his sister, Treetop, were always looking to expose the failings of other people. Maybe it ran in their blood to torment people who came through the square. He chuckled and drooled at the thought of making somebody's day miserable.

"Uncle Gil, Uncle Gil, man," he said as he tried to copy my father's emphatic diction.

Money-Roy teased people to take the attention off his lowly station in life. He was a destitute man with a loud mouth, and the very sight of him usually ruined my father's mood. I moved nearer to my father, feeling the need to be close by if Money-Roy got too abusive.

Father surprised me; he took a different approach to Money-Roy. He challenged the bum to a contest. Father tied a special knot, a running bowline, to the end of the rope that held the calf. If the drunk could duplicate the tie, he would win a ten-dollar bill.

The drunken man accepted, but he had no money to match my father's bet. Father tossed his ten-dollar bill on the ground and proceeded to make the knot around the telegraph pole. The calf at the other end of the rope watched with detachment. Father demonstrated that the loop must allow the calf to move around the pole without hitching. Once Father finished, he stepped back and waited.

Money-Roy cackled a high-pitched laugh that brought crowds of onlookers. His breath, heavy with cheap white rum, reeked in the air. He clumsily fiddled with the rope and crowed.

"See it there, Uncle Gil, man. "

The tie was a child's simple overhand twist, but my father said nothing. I thought he would give in easily, and I moved to explain that Money-Roy got it all wrong. Father roared at the calf. The animal jumped, the rope hitched, nearly taking off the calf's head. Father spat a couple of times on the ground and then gently rescued his calf.

The crowd broke up, and Money-Roy grinned sheepishly. Suddenly, he didn't seem so drunk. I picked up the ten-dollar bill and wordlessly gave it to my father. He spat his disgust a couple of times on the parched red dirt. I wanted to spit too.

Chapter 42

Once a month, my cousin Lannie came back to our district to visit his father, Uncle Buster. Lannie supervised workers at the bauxite refining plant on the other side of the island. One night at the square, I cornered him. Cousin Laine, being older and worldlier, might help me understand why folks, like Money-Roy, haunted the crossroad pestering people.

"Why is Money-Roy always troubling people at the crossroad?"

He gave a surprising response.

"There are families here who have been doing the same thing for generations."

I pictured a lineage of Money-Roy's family guarding the village gate and shaming people to stay in their place. Generations of men, like Abbot, stood drinking at the piazza. They knew everybody's disgrace and used it to shape the character of our narrow valley between the peaks.

I wondered about my family. Lannie often stopped at the crossroad to drink rum. He left after a few drinks and never got intoxicated like a common drunk. However, he visited each shop, charmed everyone, and went behind the counter to drink privately.

"Mass Lannie," I inquired respectfully, "what happened to Cousin Alonzo?"

These were sensitive family matters. Cousin Alonzo, the genius musician, had just joined the odd circle at the crossroad. Alonzo normally electrified the crowd with his saxophone, but minutes after playing, he retreated to solitude, nursing some dark despair. Money-Roy always showed up to ridicule Alonzo's failings. In the dark, Lannie shoved his face close to mine and responded.

> Full many a precious gem of purest ray serene,
> The dark unfathom'd caves of oceans bear:
> Full many a flower is born to blush unseen,
> And waste its sweetness on the desert air.

Almost before he finished the poem, Lannie bolted with the hasty strides typical of my family. Again, he loaded up on axioms and left me to figure out their meaning. I waited for months until he returned to our area. I posed my other question.

"Mass Lannie, what's the name of that poem that you quoted to me?" I barely completed the question when I got his quick answer. It was as if he anticipated a follow-up question.

"'Elegy Written in a Country Churchyard' by Thomas Gray," he shot back.

He turned to leave. Quick stride lost in the night air. I searched through Aunt Edith's old books at home, found the poem, and memorized it.

The first time I heard Cousin Alonzo play, the sound of the saxophone came on the wind across the long valley behind Uncle Buster's house. As I headed for the square, the evening turned smoky blue with his saxophone calling out to a lost love. I could not see him through the shadowed valleys, but I pictured Alonzo tormenting the keys of the sax, sending his forlorn message to his wife in England. I could not believe that someone so talented could fall so low in life.

Alonzo's saxophone told his story. The horn played a tale of a promising young musician skilled in wind and stringed instruments. He met and married the most beautiful woman in the land. They had two children, Paulette and Ray. Alonzo built a house for his family with his own hands. He also mastered carpentry and masonry.

One weekend, Alonzo left with his band to perform at a quadrille dance competition in another village. On his return, he found that his wife had left for the airport. He charted a car and raced off on the fifty-mile trip to catch her before she boarded the plane. Many people were leaving for England for a better life.

He got to the airport just as British Airways lifted his precious love to the skies. The plane roared loudly over his head, but not loud enough to drown out his anguished cry.

"Everything's gone, all gone," he wailed and bowed his head in his hands. His tears spilled past long fingers accustomed to playing many instruments. He never cried after that day.

Their partially finished house stayed that way. Like Penelope waiting for Ulysses to return, he kept watch for her. She remained in England. Their children began to grow up without their mother.

When they were a little more than toddlers, Mamma kept them on weekends while Alonzo took his band to play in quadrille dance competition in far-off villages. As he dropped off Paulette and Ray, Alonzo looked elegant in his black tuxedo suit. His neatly pressed white shirt sharply contrasted his smooth black skin. He carried a long, black case, cradling it as if he carried a precious child. I knew it held his saxophone, but he kept it closed.

I longed for him to play for us, but he never did. Perhaps he was too busy, or maybe my father prevented him from playing, lest the music remind Father of his limber years.

I heard that in his time, Father was the best quadrille dancer on the floor, but he never talked about those days. Sometimes, he jigged to a tune on the radio, but his formal dancing days were over.

We welcomed Paulette and Ray when they stayed with us. They were about our ages and were cousins from my father's side of the family. I felt their loss for not having a mother to cuddle them and play with their curly hair when they cried.

Then Paulette and Ray stopped coming on weekends. Just as suddenly, Alonzo stopped playing his saxophone. The rumor got around that Alonzo started to act bizarre, wandering around in a deep melancholic trance.

One day at the public square, he cut up his beloved saxophone with his carpenter's saw. Tool against tool, skill against skill, he seemed to enjoy the look of horror on people's faces as they witnessed the fall of their hero. He showed no concern, mumbling that he could get another instrument if he chose to. Nobody doubted him. Alonzo had crafted his first saxophone with his own hands, diligently carving it from bamboo. Such was the power of his legend.

Months later, at some unknown signal, Alonzo shed the gloom and switched to his other profession as a carpenter. Sometimes the death of a villager prompted the switch. The grieving family needed his skill to form the casket from the heartwood of the cedar tree. Alonzo patiently planed the rough boards to reveal the dark, red interior of the heartwood. His long fingers coaxed life from the plank, and people came to look over his shoulder, seeing that this man possessed some special ability with the wood.

The talented Alonzo didn't quite belong with the desperate men at the crossroad, but he drew a crowd quicker than anyone could. The dark tale of his wife leaving him alone with two infants persisted.

After his wife left him, he wandered in and out of melancholia like someone left ajar a door for him to walk in and out as he saw fit. As I tried to understand his torment, a poem of empathy came to my mind.

COUSIN ALONZO

The call of your sax rising
and cresting too soon,
and the crowd is hungry for more
of the breath from your lips.
Horn man's breath
that you would prefer to be on the face of a
woman who has left the sound of the beat.

Heartbeat that still aches above the drums,
beyond time.
Distance still does not replace the space,
as long fingers play fickle tunes
seeking to abate the flow,
the need to be close,
away from the embrace that this crowd offers,
but instead comes to take some salve
for their longings, that they see in your pain.

You play,
each note smelling of all the days
latched on to loneliness.
You play to soften the hole
that you guard and do not seek to fill,
and all in synchrony shed a mutual tear.

And still they do not know why they weep
with you, horn man,
for they see your pain as your failing
And it makes you fit
with their unreachable dreams

Your sax smashes the air
that traps them in tranquil acceptance
of discarded paths.
And you capture their dreams, for an instant;
you play their own need to create.
You hold them at will.
Cradling, toying, mocking!

You make them dream again.
Your full eyes, flashing with enviable sweet passion.
They push for more, forgetting your pain,
and you play, forgetting too.

You watch them maddened
halfway between the acceptance
of their own hurt
and the memory of their dreams
discarded like old clothes.

Someone sticks a microphone in the throat of your
sax and broadcasts your longings.
And they dance, because you mask your grief
and they think maybe you are healed.

When you let them go
to prime your horn with distilled spirits,
They remember that you are crazy
and feel the space of living with forgotten dreams,
and the numbness of acceptance.
Their lives return to break the trance of your music.

And as you forget
to feel their pain,
the music leaves with them.
Your horn tries to call
"Come back! Come back!"
For your own morbidity looms
close to the brooding look on your forehead.

A croak from your stalling instrument brings
those who come to ridicule.
They pester you with your failings,
and you cast aside your horn
and retreat to the safety of melancholia.

You mope behind the departing crowd
stealing company with the shadows,
fearful to go home
where no trace of perfume lingers,
and no tufts of curly hair awaits
your exploration.

Chapter 43

Mr. Rampart's green Buick sedan crept up the winding road to our school. The car bounced softly as it crested the hill and creaked to a stop. The mustached man flaunted a mop of wavy hair that hung down to mutton-chop sideburns. Both his hair and the mustache were an unruly sea of salt and pepper. His complexion and facial detail marked his mixed ancestry of African, European, and possibly East Indian.

He looked past the curious stares of my schoolmates with the all-knowing eyes of a sage. Mr. Rampart, an education inspector, came to observe the teachers. The staff anxiously scurried the students to their classrooms.

Mr. Rampart took over the headmaster's class and proceeded to check our understanding of geometry. He taught masterfully in front of the classroom. Mr. Beastly slipped to the back of the class, pacing uneasily. His beady eyes flickered brightly with the trapped look he exhibited when something bothered him.

None of the students offered to answer Mr. Rampart's questions, so I felt that I needed to make the principal look good. I raised my hand and answered. Repeatedly the inspector smiled his affirmation. Then we came to angles. Right angles I knew, but he began to draw other angles that I didn't know. I made up an answer. Since right angles were ninety degrees, then other angles must be *left* angles, I reasoned. I raised my hand and gave my confident *left angle* answer.

The smile ran off Mr. Rampart's face like the first rain runs off the ground after the dry season. The lines of smiles on the corner of his eyes straightened out. He glared at the headmaster, motioning him aside. Head to head, they conversed quietly behind the class.

Mr. Beastly dropped his eyes and fixated on his shoes. He seemed contrite, and I liked him in that posture. In turn, I surely would feel the Scorpion's sting from the humiliated headmaster's belt. I should have never tried to save his face.

After Mr. Rampart left, Mr. Beastly stormed to the front of the class. He seemed energized to redeem himself. He drew neat figures on the board and patiently explained how to measure the angles.

He rarely relaxed when he taught, but now he smiled and looked in my direction with a bit of kindness. The articulate man standing in front of the class amazed us. I took notes as fast as I could, eager to learn more about acute, obtuse, and corresponding angles.

After he wrapped up the lesson, the class remained unusually quiet; not that we ever got noisy, since we were terrified of his wrath. Mr. Beastly got past something fierce inside him, and once he showed his human side, he was a fine teacher. He wandered away leaving his Scorpion strap still sitting on his desk. I never got the beating I so dreaded.

Chapter 44

Father's eyes turned baby blue, matching the color of his favorite dress shirt. I knew he was fighting back tears. He kept bouncing from foot to foot in a nervous, happy dance. Salaman, the only man with a newspaper told him good news. Father abandoned the fields, hurried to the crossroad, and borrowed a newspaper to "see it with his own eyes."

He opened the paper and brought it over to where I lay ill in bed.

"Dan-Dan, you passed your exam," his voice cracked as he fought back tears.

I had passed the revered Common Entrance Exam and won a full scholarship to any of Jamaica's elite high schools. It had been years since a boy in our community passed this scholarship examination. This was the best gift any child could give to his or her parents.

"Tell me what you want," he said. "I will give you anything".

It shocked me to see this hardened man turn soft and supple to humbly pay tribute to me. His normal, stony exterior cracked to reveal tenderness. I wanted to tell him that I just wished to make my family proud. Secretly, I wished that my award would cause Father to walk through the crossroad indifferent to the contempt that idlers heaped on him.

"I don't want anything, Papa," I muttered through the bandaged poultice that wrapped my face and kept my cheeks from swelling past my ears.

I suffered from mumps and a fever that came with the disease. The fluids from the infection drained into my mouth, leaving a nauseating taste. My family treated all childhood illness with home remedies and lots of love and attention from Dr. Gentles, my mother. This time, she gave me a dosage of honey and lime juice. I toyed with a little flask of the mixture as Father watched.

It made me happy to see my father filled with pride. My parents held their marriage together waiting "'till the children are past the worst." I barely felt ill. I felt powerful. I gave them a reason to be happy.

Father leaned against the bulletwood door of the tiny room. He wrapped his strong hand over the top of the door and pulled himself upright. His dress felt hat covered his bald dome and most of the thin flecks of wavy hair. His presence filled the room with energy, yet he seemed frustrated that he could do nothing to aid my present condition. Abruptly, he left to get Mamma. She knew how to heal with her gentle touch and her unending patience.

I returned to elementary school about a week later, still weak from the infection. As I walked through the crossroad, people greeted me with wordless affection. They stared at me as if it made them feel good just to see me. When I passed the infant school, the teacher ran out, pumped my hand, and gave a congratulation speech. It was the first time she had ever spoken to me. Unsure how to respond, I gave her what my aunt called "the Evangelist" smile.

I saw Mr. Beastly helping a band of boys move desks as I approached the elementary school. He might switch mood as suddenly as dark clouds rage over the mountains, so I approached cautiously.

"Manning." He always used my last name. "You are feeling better."

A rare smile cracked his features. His face broke into little uncertain pieces that completely disarmed him. He pressed my hand in a warm handshake. The hand that once slapped my face motioned well done. I read a little of his soul as he clasped my hand, but he remained a tortured man, uneasy with his demons.

I expected him to savor the moment with me. As the only scholarship recipient from five local schools in the mountain, I deserved a *go forth* pronouncement. He had to know I taught half the class every time he beat them senseless. It takes more than a beating to teach children.

At least, he could bless my journey with the traveler's *walk good* proclamation. As he strode by, I sensed that, despite his education, he did not possess a kind word. For the first time in my six years at this school, I felt him step aside so that I could move on.

The group of boys broke as he strode through the crowd. He was a moody man with a temper as unpredictable as a sudden thunderstorm sweeping over the mountain and into our valley. Without warning he might pounce on an unsuspecting boy and slap him senseless.

I skipped awkwardly to avoid the boys stepping on my new, white puss-crepe shoes. They were Aunt Edith's reward for my scholarship. She always encouraged academic excellence.

The shoes looked unnaturally clean above the thin film of red dust covering floor. I was the only one wearing shoes but soon the soil would stain these white shoes a dirty cinnamon-red. Today I would enjoy them. I walked on air. ✓

Part 3: Coming of Age

Chapter 45

On a September morning, Father strode with me to the crossroad to catch the bus to town. He stared down the idlers waiting to make fun of his peculiarities, but nobody teased him. In a community with a high percentage of illiterate folks, the father of a son with a full academic scholarship to the best school in town earned a short reprieve.

In town, the bus dropped us off by the side of the road, and we walked the half mile up to my new school. Rows of royal palms lined the walkway up to the old plantation house used for administration. The building, a relic of the colonial era, still had a bulletwood shingle roof bleached white from a century of weathering.

Inside, a restored living room served as a waiting area. The polished wooden floor reflected every bit of light from a brightly lit chandelier. As we walked across the floor, a hollow echo sounded from the cellar below.

Father took a prominent seat next to the principal's office, crossed his legs, and waited. Even though we traveled fifteen miles to the school, we were first to arrive. He never went anywhere late.

A woman walked in with her son and took a seat next to us. Father struck up a conversation with her. He told her he felt proud I'd earned a scholarship to this exclusive high school. She listened and nodded. I turned red from his boasting, and I wished I could leave, but the room filled up quickly.

Father held up well-manicured fingers as he gestured at the woman. I wondered how he always kept his hands so clean and free from the scars and calluses that were the trademark of his life as a farmer.

The woman latched on to his every word.

"You must be a proud man. He looks just like you," she offered, projecting her voice across the room.

A few people raised their eyebrows, and the room fell silent. I longed for the registration to end so I could return to the quiet, unceremonious people of the distant hills.

After enrolling, we climbed the wooden stairs to purchase books on the second-floor bookstore. The school chaplain ran the bookstore. Previously, I had seen him in my neighborhood ministering to the Refuge Anglican Church with the big bell that tolled out the passing of local souls.

A relic of the English three-hundred-year rule of the island, the high and mighty minister seldom spoke to the locals. Safe and secure behind the counter of the bookstore, he waved a finger and glared above his brown, horn-rimmed spectacles.

"Now, you can only purchase complete sets of books, you see. If you desire individual books, I'd rather you wait until later."

None of the parents seemed bothered by his distance. Father ran to the head of the line. He bought the full set without blinking an eye. Aunt Edith, a stickler for education, had given him the money. We were always short of money, so I tried to tell Father that my older sisters owned some of the books back home, but he disregarded me. He despised waiting on lines.

We grabbed the set of books and scrambled toward the bus stop at the town center. Even at seventy-two years old, Father summoned the energy to walk as fast as my twelve-year-old legs.

Chapter 46

On Saturday before school, Father commanded the barber to shake off his usual twitches and come to my house and give me a fresh haircut. With a steady hand, the barber trimmed by hair and meticulously shaved my hairline.

The following Monday morning I struggled to knot the maroon necktie — the last touch to my brand-new khaki school uniform. The necktie gave me distinction as I boarded the bus. Nobody else wore a tie. By leaving the village on a scholarship to town, I already enjoyed a greater level of success than my peers.

At the end of my first day, I blended in with a pack of boys walking to town. They knew all the shortcuts, and I craved to learn these new ways. Hugh, the most popular boy in the class, led the pack. His older brother captained the football team, and the younger boy reveled in his big brother's fame.

All the girls showered Hugh with affection as if he were the coolest boy in school. His family owned a hardware store, and that gave him claim to a higher station in life. Boys followed him wherever he went. Hugh liked me instantly, and I walked with his group and quietly observed how folks in town behaved. He shortened my last name to Manny, and everyone started calling me that.

On one of the back roads, I ran into Ellen, the daughter of Miss Mattie, the local shopkeeper in the village. Ellen was the big sister of my elementary classroom companion, Ricky, and she had advised me to choose this high school.

I greeted her with warmth, happy to see a familiar face in this sea of strangers. Back home in the village, a flock of girls always trailed her as if she were a princess, but in town, not a soul followed her. She glanced nervously at the pack of boys and cautioned.

"Don't let them know you are from Mocho."

Ellen hurried away before I could ask for an explanation.

Puzzled, I lost my smile and slithered to the back of the group. I never knew I came from Mocho. I thought I lived in the village of Foga, next to the Brickman crossroad. How could the world scorn me because of where I came from?

I learned about Mocho from Hugh the next day in woodworking class. We never really used wood in the class, but instead we learned about lettering and technical drawing. The teacher, a light-brown man, liked to dress up in immaculately pressed clothes. As he opened his mouth to teach, Hugh set upon him.

"Hee, hee, Mocho Man. Peenie Wallie, backward people." He pointed a finger and raised his voice to a singing, mocking tone.

"Look, look, at the Mocho Man," he chided, his voice steeped in contempt and pungent with the acrid support of cultural stereotyping.

Mocho, I learned, was the worst place on earth. Uncivilized people lived in Mocho. They had no right to be among city people because they came from a backward, lowly place.

Hugh sat behind me, and I suffered in silence lest he pounce on me next. He ignored me and continued to berate the teacher. Nobody laughed, but he never shut up. At that moment, I saw the value in Ellen's advice. I decided to keep it a secret that I came from Mocho. Shame followed me here too.

Mr. River, the teacher, turned his back on the boy and tried to shut him out, but Hugh rambled like a transistor radio that never ran out of batteries. Occasionally the teacher turned and glared at the tormentor, but he never found the right words to shut the boy up. I knew that Mr. River came from a prominent family in Mocho, but here in town he was something inferior.

The teacher stayed behind the safety of his desk, keeping distance between himself and the boy. Most of the other boys bent their heads and copied the beautiful letters from the board. My hands shook a little as I struggled with the tension in the class.

Day after day, the torment continued, and I wondered about the power of one student over an entire class. I thought of elementary school when Mr. Beastly ruled with the power of his Scorpion belt. For a moment, I longed for that disciplined environment.

Gradually, I understood Ellen's warning. I lived on the Mocho Mountain range, and that made me a Mocho Man. Outside the classroom window, the Mocho Mountains stood bold and defiant, and shadowed in part by rain clouds. Rain sustained the food that fed my family. We sent our surplus to the market to feed the families of this parched, unfriendly town. Still, I found no peace with this mountain that gave its name so painfully to the children of its soil.

Beneath its canopies, Father's nimble fingers were wrapping the yam vines around the long poles that pointed at the clouds and beckoned for rain. He had already broken his first morning sweat and drunk a quart of water from the huge, white enamel mug. Soon he would stop for an early lunch of boiled yams, breadfruit, and codfish stewed in home-made coconut oil.

Mr. River's voice broke through as he explained how to use the divider to center the heading on the paper.

"Only the tiny ticks of the divider should be left on your paper."

He held up his right thumb and forefinger, pinched together to emphasize how tiny the marks ought to be made. With his other hand, he daintily pointed at the tiny tip of the divider. Clumsily I stabbed my paper with my divider.

Unused to struggling with my work, I tried smooth out the blemishes on the paper. No good. I shot a glance up at the hills again. I could see Mamma in the kitchen grating sweet potatoes. Her hands struck a regular rhythm as she slid the potatoes across the metal barbs of the grater. She could grate a pan of potatoes without looking at the grater. As she worked, her eyes went somewhere soft, away from the toil and the smoke-filled kitchen.

Next, she grated a coconut, mixed it in hot water, and extracted the juice by straining the shredded material through a sieve. Mamma was getting ready to bake a sweet potato pudding, and one taste of her pastries sweetened life.

Someone rang a bell to signal the end of class. My paper gleamed back at me, white and forbidding. Except for the border around the page, I'd done nothing. I glanced at the work of the other boys around me. Neat geometric figures filled their pages. Mr. River never collected anything to grade, and I never attempted any of his work.

After school, heeding Ellen's advice, I split off from the group and quietly waited for the vehicle to take me home to Mocho's safe hills.

Chapter 47

The summer after my first year in high school, my sisters Hazel and Jan decided it was time for me spend a week in the junior Christian camp. Every summer they went to the senior camp. The missionary host at the camp charmed them, and they made new friends from all over the island. I'd never left home for a night, and now they expected me to last a week in the big city? My sisters helped me pack.

I had trouble adjusting to camp and city life. I longed for the predictable stillness that prevailed over my childhood valleys. Most of all, I missed Mamma's tireless, comforting smiles and her bedtime stories. One night, I became so homesick that I cried silently before I went to sleep. I made sure that nobody in the dormitory saw my tears. The other boys at the camp seemed perfectly happy, and I never wanted to be the crybaby. Normally the last one to fall asleep, I tossed and turned, listening to a roomful of boys with crude bedtime rituals.

The darlings of the camp were two brothers from England, and with their fine accents, they got all the attention. Althea, the daughter of one of the white American missionaries in the camp, lavished the boys with attention. I watched them giggling and soaking up her warmth. Althea always walked by without looking at me. I craved her attention, and I spent my spare time thinking of a way to get her to notice me.

One night after an ice-cream social, we were getting ready for bed when I saw Althea outside the window. The rising moon outlined her face as she charmed the other counselors. I plucked up my courage and called her over to the window where I could tell her the secret, I saved for her. She walked over, light as a feather and full of confidence.

"Althea," I whispered, "You may have seen me staring at you, but I can't help it."

Her mouth popped open, and she looked me over. The moon above shone bright as her face as she tiptoed backward away from the window. All the while, she kept her eyes on me. I locked her in my gaze and stood motionless until she walked past the shadow of the huge guangu tree and back to the cafeteria.

When she got back to her group, she spoke in a hushed voice.

"You heard what my boyfriend Manning just said to me?" Her soft voice carried across the distance to where I remained at the window.

She repeated what I'd said to the other counselors, and they sat around talking in low tones. The power of words to change people's perception surprised me. Althea did not even know my first name, but she knew my older sisters. Flush with the warmth of the encounter, I went to bed and slept soundly.

When I saw her the next day, we were unsure how to relate to each other. At fifteen, she was a couple years older, and blessed with all that made her a woman. As a late bloomer, I'd just started puberty.

Nightly, as we walked to the campfire, she let me hold her hand. She smelled like lavender and fresh grasslands rolling in the breeze. I prayed for the night to drift by slowly, but time flew.

At the end of the week, I won the runner-up model camper. My attempt to adjust to life in the dormitories received more acclaim that I imagined. I suspected they selected me because the camp counselors liked my sisters, Hazel and Jan.

For the remainder of the camp, I stole her attention from the boys with the fine English accent. When camp concluded, we were pen pals for a while, but it became obvious that she was too mature for me.

When Hazel returned from senior summer camp, she began organizing trips to visit other churches at their conventions. I saw some of the girls from camp. We renewed acquaintances, exchanged addresses, and pledged to write to each other. Althea attended all the meetings. She smiled sweetly as ever, but a male companion planted himself by her side. I felt happy to talk to the fine teenage girls my own age.

Chapter 48

People at our church functions ignored the barriers between country and town folks. In the autumn, I returned to school and tried to blend in, but children in the plains spotted a Mocho man faster than I could slip on the country bus. They even cursed the Mocho bus that took us over the dusty roads to the asphalt roads in town.

Though they ate the food from our farms in Mocho, town folks walked around our vehicles. They despised the passengers as much as they did the layers of red dirt on the bus. The red soil held bauxite, one of most valuable minerals in the western hemisphere, but townsfolk were too preoccupied with city lights to value red dirt.

During my second year in high school, a new boy, Larry, joined our class. He spewed his hate for Mocho people. If my shoes were dirty, he blamed it on me being Mocho. If he saw me in the bathroom, he commented on my Mocho-man anatomy. He even labeled my complexion "as red as the Mocho dirt." The boy had a gift for assigning a derisive nickname and gave me the name Mocho Manny. It stuck.

Larry ridiculed anyone, including the prettiest girl in class. On the surface, the girls appeared to enjoy his company, but he never showed any affection for any of them. I did not know whether girls found him attractive or they wanted to avoid his foul temperament.

The boy tormentor always took the offensive as if blocking anyone from probing his secrets. Even though he harassed me, I never got angry enough to fight him. A dirty fighter, he seemed bigger and meaner. One day my friend Longers challenged him to stop pestering me. Larry picked up a stick and smashed Longers on his wrist. He chuckled at the sight of blood dripping from my friend's arm.

Back in elementary school, I'd beat up the school bully and I wanted to beat up Larry. As the only boy from Mocho, I felt I could never win a fight against the label. I found no reason to compete with someone who effused such genuine pleasure for inflicting misery on others. Sometimes, though, I felt like a coward for avoiding a fight with him.

A mere ten miles away, the foothills of the Mocho Mountains towered, and they were constant evidence of my roots. Back in the village, I never mentioned that town folks thought so little of us, but I valued the love and support waiting for me back there among the trees. I held their trust sacred. Few boys from my district ever saw the insides of a city high school, so I avoided getting in trouble for fighting in school. This tormentor, Larry, was a thorny bush around which I made a wide detour.

Chapter 49

After school, I hurried to the bus stop to catch the minivan home. A man told me that my grown-up older brother Phil and my mother were trying to find me. Phil left home to live in the big city when I was a baby. Occasionally, he drove down to the country to visit Mamma. He owned a souped-up Ford with a racing engine, and I yearned to ride in it and feel the power. I wondered what brought him to the area. He hardly left the big city.

I looked around for Mamma and Phil, but they were gone. Mamma was supposed to be in the city visiting Hazel in the hospital. My sister suddenly got sick, turning yellow with jaundice, and a doctor in town rushed her to a hospital in the big city.

I gave up trying to find them and got on the minivan for the more than hour-long ride home. Near to the crossroad, the minivan drove past a group of girls walking home from the local secondary school. Merle led the pack.

I grew up with Merle and her sisters in church. Together we performed in the church choir, and the girls sang like angels. Merle waved at me as I passed and tried to shout a warning to me. Her eyes flashed like the warner woman, Maddah, when she came to the village square to deliver a dreadful omen. The minivan drove past her, and she kept gesticulating and pointing at me.

As I stepped off the van at the crossroad, Abbot struck me with the news. He knew everything that happened in the village, and if you vexed him, he put you in your place. He still scorned me because years ago, I'd mocked his drunkenness. Rum took the vigor from his glare, but still a scorpion, he could sting if prodded from his lair.

His hawk eyes flared, and the rum-ball bobbed as if something got caught in his throat, but he got it out.

"Bwoy you don't know that you sister dead?"

Hazel had passed away in the hospital the night before. Abbot gauged my reaction. I was too old to cry openly, but not quite a stoic man of the village. I could never tell if Abbot was drunk or just having trouble with his own grief. Wordlessly, I walked past him. I swallowed my tears and he his Adam's apple.

The hills closed in, and the narrow valley darkened as I walked home. People got out of my way, afraid that my malady would spread to them and snatch their loved ones. A gray blanket hung over the valley.

When I got home, Phil had left for the city. He took Mamma home and left me to find my way home on the minivan. Abbot, with his rum for tears, broke the news of my sister's passing. Mamma and Papa were in shock. They rallied us for dinner, and we stared at our plates.

Once more, Father reached under the cellar and retrieved the cedar boards that he preserved so carefully. This time it was for someone whom we least expected. The village carpenters made a coffin from the boards, and like Uncle Mack's, the polished wood glowed splendidly.

Mamma made my sister's final outfit. She sewed white lace and trims to a purple dress.

"The color of royalty," she mused as she snipped the tread from the last stitch. She stopped sewing clothes after that dress.

Uncle Buster abandoned his usual distance toward my father and offered his jeep to return my sister's remains from the funeral parlor. Even though he had a driver, Uncle drove the Land Rover on the long journey to bring my sister home.

When he arrived at the church, Buster wore his finest dark suit. A stare as impassive as a cedarwood replaced his charming smile. Wordlessly, he delivered the autopsy report to Mamma. She read aloud.

"Viral infection of the liver."

Nobody knew what that meant. A traveling dental technician working under the guise of a dentist had recently completed dental work on Hazel. The experience left her drained. She started to recover her zest for life when she suddenly got ill.

Hazel's usual fighting spirit was gone from the limp form in the casket. Only her brave soul knew how to confront my father when he quarreled with Mamma.

The white American missionaries came from Kingston for the funeral. The father flashed a disarming smile as he ran his fingers through a full head of silver hair. His wife marched next to him, hunting for the right words to say. I often imitated her operatic soprano voice to amuse my siblings. That thought now gave me no cheer.

Their two children always attended church functions with them. If you closed your eyes and listened to their voices, they sounded just like locals; unless you looked in their blue eyes or touched their blond hair.

Hazel had just finished a successful year of summer camp with them. She emerged as a promising youth leader.

Althea traveled with the missionaries. She looked more grownup since I'd last seen her. I refused her offer to go back inside the church and sit with her. She shook her head, looked at me with big sad eyes, and left. I placed one foot inside the door, afraid to leave and afraid to stay.

No one put a hand on my shoulder and gave me permission to cry. I fought the urge to cry and gulped my grief in choking lumps. The lumps hurt all the way down, fell in an empty space in my gut, and stayed there for a long time. I felt like Abbot, gulping his lumps of grief.

"That little bwoy is going to be a tough man," one of the men outside the church said with pride as they saw my tearless face. I tried to fit in with the men of my neighborhood. They only mourned after they drank a bottle of rum. With the devil soup, they could lose inhibitions and blame it on the rum. At thirteen years old, I never drank rum.

I poked my head in the church. Inside, a young man from camp sang his final dedication to my sister. He strained to keep his beautiful tenor from cracking. The mostly female mourners patiently saw him through his stops and starts until he finished. He showed his love for my sister with more courage than I possessed.

Father, like most of the men in the village, avoided funeral services. I understood his absence from the church because I knew he waited at the graveside. After the church services, I rode in the missionary's van to the burial site. I found no way to express my unbearable grief, so I kept it inside as I had learned from the men in my neighborhood. My heart turned to stone.

My father arrived at the graveside before anyone. He supervised the digging of the grave, the building of the coffin, and all the rituals of a funeral. He showed no public grief.

Father kept a steady hand on the rope as they lowered my sister into the ground. When they covered her up, he took the rope and wound it tightly around his waist. He looked gaunt as a shadow with the rope wrapping him in bands from chest to buttocks.

I feared his eccentric behavior lest it spread to me. I did not yet know that dozens of nerves meet at the navel point. If you can suppress this seat of emotion, you can restrain your immediate need to grieve. In time, I understood the local saying, "band you belly lest you weep."

With my belt tightened around my waist, I returned to school in the plains. No one seemed to notice that I was gone for two weeks. I found a quiet place and stared back at the Mocho Mountains.

Chapter 50

Feeling vulnerable after Hazel's passing, Mamma went to the doctor for a checkup. They found *something* and the doctor sent her to the city for follow-up treatments. When she returned home, she resumed her labor at the fireside, cooking our meals. The drudgery of bringing us up filled her life with burdensome tasks. For decades, she endured the smoke-filled kitchen without complaint, but I saw a change in her. Losing a daughter in the prime of life shook her confidence.

I kept on the lookout for an opportunity to do my bit and make life easier for Mamma. Sometimes the firewood that Father brought home produced an offensive smoke as Mamma cooked at the fireplace. Her eyes turned red and irritated. I grew tired of seeing her suffer because my aging father lacked the strength to carry quality firewood from the distant hills.

At one time, we used a wood-burning stove with the name *Caledonia Modern Dover* brazed across the front. There was nothing modern about this behemoth, wrought iron stove. An old block wood replaced the missing two of four legs. With its four burners and ample oven space, it occupied half of the kitchen wall.

No other household possessed a stove equal to this relic of my family's former standing in the community. For years, Mamma baked her black fruitcakes in the oven, and I liked when she occasionally cooked on the stovetop. Whenever she cooked on the open fire, smoke swirled all over the kitchen, but the wood stove's chimney quickly funneled the fumes outside.

One day she found a nest of scorpions prowling inside the oven. Scorpions haunted dark, crumbling, musty old places such as the wrought iron stove. The image of the pests lying in wait ruined the atmosphere in our kitchen. I came home one afternoon, and the stove was gone. Our old stove symbolized that we were a cut above the ordinary, but I preferred getting rid of the scorpions in my life.

Every weekend since I could walk without tripping, Father towed me to the woodlands to find firewood. Before he left, he sharpened the axe to a wicked-looking, white edge.

"Touch the edge, you lose a finger, man," he warned.

Father knew all the trees in the forest, and I quizzed him about their names. I memorized the names of the trees on our weekly trips into the woodland.

"What kind of tree is that?" I questioned repeatedly. He wanted firewood instead of naming live trees, and I became a nuisance.

"Green tree," he replied. He'd had enough of my questions, but I knew the tree anyway, the wild olive in its deciduous stage.

When I turned fourteen, I felt that I could do a better job than my aging father. I grabbed the axe and tramped to the woodlands behind Uncle Mack's house. The bauxite company delayed mining his land and, in the meantime, we farmed on the property.

A small, dried tree made the perfect target. I chopped it down, trimmed off the smaller branches, and lifted the log to my shoulder as my father did for many years. I was surprised how strong I felt and how well the log balanced on my shoulder. I placed the axe handle on my other shoulder and used it as a lever to lessen the strain.

Loaded down, I walked home. Just before I climbed the last hill to our house, I stopped to catch my breath. I wanted to stride into the yard bearing the weight of the load like a man. After my breather, I picked up the log and climbed the hill. When I passed the kitchen, I tossed the log with one flick of the shoulder. It crashed to the ground announcing that *man* brought fuel home to cook dinner. I made my most powerful noise thus far in my household.

When Father arrived home with freshly harvested food, I had already chopped the log into smaller pieces for the fire. For years, I watched him split the hardwood logs, but he never showed me how to swing the axe. He always steered me away from hard toil on the farm. He wanted me to do well in school and avoid donkeywork.

Father said nothing to me about the pile of split logs. He just lost the job of providing the fuel for our home. In time, the task became easier as I organized a pack of boys my age to chop wood for our separate households.

While he waited turns at swinging the axe, one of the teens entertained us with stories about the people in our area. He mastered local tradition of turning people into lively caricatures. Most of the time, the jokes were about folks who fell on hard times. I frowned on these tales, even though I faked a chuckle. Human suffering did not entertain me.

Mamma made sure we valued all human life. She disliked *carry-down artists*, people who dragged others down. She welcomed anyone who returned to the community after they lost out on life beyond the village.

Moreover, my family was often subjected to public ridicule because nobody understood why my father walked so fast, worked so hard, and why he never tolerated slothful people. The jokes ran hollow. People made fun of the unfortunate to divert attention away from their own plight. We were all stuck on the side of a mountain with people whose customs had changed little since olden days.

In between stories, I urged the boys to wield the axe. I disliked chopping wood, but I feared Father might reclaim the job. I liked the fact that Mamma stopped complaining about the quality of the kindling.

Taking over one of Father's many tough jobs earned me a passage to manhood. On a farm, everyone works. My parents gradually gave me the freedom to chart whatever course I saw fit. At fourteen, I was more educated than they were. They expected me to make the right choices.

Chapter 51

Brown dusk was the short-lived period before shadows flooded our valley. The numerous peaks never allowed a long descent of the sun and a trail of red skies at sunset. Normally, the sun quickly dropped beyond one of the hills, and evening turned brown, then black. I saw Angie as "brown dusk" lost out to the moon rising above the village square.

Miles away from home, Angie came to buy a last-minute item from Miss Mattie's shop. In the moonlight, her pink dress stopped high enough to expose appealing thighs. She had grown up. Curves replaced her prior slender form. I offered to walk her home, half expecting her to refuse. She accepted with an easygoing charm. Her younger sister plodded slowly behind, eying us.

Angie and I were classmates back in Mr. Beastly's elementary school, but when she went to Mocho secondary, she escaped the headmaster's fury. Since I traveled to school in town every day, I had not seen her in a long time.

I whistled for my friend Ronny as we walked past his house. Ronny and I had our own coded whistle to recognize each other in the dark. We knew each other well.

For years we sat side-by-side on the bulletwood bench in church. As one, we repented our sins and laughed at Uncle Buster's bad sermons. In the choir, we stood together and sang at churches across the island. His singing came from a place of unfettered joy.

Always willing to follow my lead, he came quickly. I asked him to escort Angie's sister. He strolled beside her, silent and protecting.

As we wandered up and down the slopes, Angie chatted about a legend associated with her new school. Maddah, the warner woman from the nearby village, predicted that the school would come to a sudden, tragic end. Her warnings were on the lips of every child because her premonitions always came true.

"When a Doctor Bird flies into the school with a fish in its beak, the school will sink under water! Beware, Beware! Mmhmm, Mmhmm."

The Doctor Bird, the revered hummingbird, is Jamaica's National Bird. The hummingbird inserts its long needle-like beak into flowers to feed on nectar. With its lengthy tail feathers extended, its flight is dramatic and of singular beauty.

Hummingbirds never feed on fish, and no surface water existed in our porous limestone topography. A flood at the school was as unlikely as the hummingbird catching a fish.

Though improbable, not a soul dismissed the powerful symbolism of the bird bringing the fish. Water must follow. While they were in school, Angie and her classmates kept watch for the doctor bird.

I held on to Angie's hand, urged her to dismiss the seer's words, and forget about school. As we strode up to my house, I stopped and picked a few of the last fruits of the orange season. The last fruits were always the sweetest.

The citrus season just ended, but Father saved one tree filled with navel oranges for Phil and our grown-up brothers from "town." The longer they stayed on the tree, the sweeter and more tempting they got.

"Leave them alone," Father decreed.

We, the younger children, were forbidden from eating these special fruits. Father was asleep as I used my pocketknife to peel a few of the juicy oranges. We tasted the sweetness and smiled.

Moonlight flooded the valley, revealing the green hue of the trees. I wrapped my arm around Angie's waist and tried to sidestep her toes. Hugging and walking was a new skill for me, and inadvertently, I stepped on her toes with my flip-flops. We chuckled and snuggled closer.

From the valley below our house, fragrance from the rose-apple tree flooded the air. During the day, bees and hummingbirds flocked to the sweet, scented flowers, nudging a flight of the delicate petals to the earth.

Next to the rose-apple tree, great buttress roots created shadows under the cedar trees beside Sonny's mother grave. The shadows, large enough to conceal a man, enshrined the unsolved mysteries of the woman's passing. Even as the dark enclaves offered secrecy, Isaiah's ghostly presence still hung over the place. Angie nestled closer.

The open road remained too bright for my first kiss. Gently I pulled Angie toward me and plunged in the shadows under the tree. She exhaled gently and snuggled closer. I felt her body pressed against mine, contoured and firm. The leaves parted as the cedar tree swayed in a light breeze that rocked the pinnacle. Softly as the falling blossoms from a rose-apple tree, a glimmer of light fell on her rosy lips.

Her soft scent blended with the rose-apple blooms as I found her lips. They were supple and yielding, sweet like the forbidden fruits we just tasted.

I paused to catch my breath and then wrapped my arms tighter and checked if the sweet taste lingered on her lips. Warmth washed away any taste of the fruit. She pulled away gently and stepped back in the moonlight. We still needed to walk a mile to her home.

We strolled through a lonely, forbidden track that led to the haunted paths of Thatch Walk. As a little boy, I passed over this same route on the way to Mountain with my father. These trips long ago cured me of any fear of the dark. Nothing moved as we walked between the quiet, solitary hills.

The moon dropped our shadows at our feet. I searched for my toes in the dark, feeling like I was walking in the clouds. The night brought on a reflective mood. Our teenage lives were bursting with possibilities yet fleeting as a stolen kiss beneath a ghost tree.

When we got to Angie's grandma's house, we were a close foursome, pressed together and talking in hushed voices. Teens were supposed to be indoors getting ready for school the next day. The girls whispered good night and tiptoed away. Grandma disapproved of boys coming to her house at night.

Ronny and I stopped a couple yards from the door and watched as they blended with the shadows where the house blocked out the peering eyes of the moon. Angie gently pushed open the unlocked door. She closed it softly. No hint of activity came from inside.

The parting left a void that Ronny could not fill. He and I switched roles. The restless one, I often expressed my thought aloud. He was usually quiet as the distant hills. Now he wanted to talk. I ignored him.

I'd kissed a girl for the first time, and she had responded to my own stirrings. A sense of individuality awakened in me. It gave me a license to explore my own emotions away from the limits of my household. Some of the clouds that surrounded me since the passing of my sister began to lift away.

On the way back, we passed the cedar tree where Angie and I paused to kiss. The moon seemed ready to slip behind Isaiah's hill and shadows filled the valley. The legend of the lizards haunting the cedar trees meant nothing. I could only think of Angie's sweet kiss on my lips.

Chapter 52

Every morning Father's holler shattered my favorite morning dream, rousing me up to get ready for school. Daylight Saving Time, the bane of an industrialized society visited upon an island people, forced people to get up one hour earlier in the dark. Mornings were my favorite time to steer my dream wherever I wanted. I ignored Father and tried to jump back into my dream, but his call grew louder and more distressing, ruining my slumber. I hated him for snatching me from my fantasies. Just to placate him, I fumbled in the dark and dressed for the long ride to school.

Designed to help save fuel in the energy crisis of the 1970s, Daylight Savings Time rankled everyone. We burned wood for fuel and gained nothing by getting up early, braving the dark, and going to work. Daylight Saving Time reminded people of the island's painful past, when our foreparents suffered through forced servitude from sunup to sundown. Folks cynically called this attempt at clock management, "Daylight-Slaving Time."

Father, the exception, always rose before the rooster's crow signaled dawn. He easily adjusted to the new schedule. The day they turned clocks back, he grabbed his machete, stepped outside into the dark, and walked me to the bus stop.

As we headed for the crossroad, I wondered why he wanted to accompany me. For years, I'd walked by myself. Our trudges up to Mountain long ago cured me of any fear of the dark. Certainly, I'd never boarded the minivan in the darkness of Daylight-Saving Time, but few got up this early.

Father cradled the handle of the machete while the back of the blade nestled against his shoulder like the barrel of a rifle. The fading light of a full moon dying in the west flicked the top of the nearby hills. Sometimes moonlight sneaked between two peaks and bathed a slope in silver light, but the darkness of the night remained unchecked.

As we walked to the square, a comet watched us from the heavens. Its long tail blazed across the sky. No one could explain this unusual stellar event, but folks marveled about its remarkable brilliance.

Mamma taught my siblings and me a little about astronomy. She pointed out the Big Dipper and the Little Dipper, and even taught us a poem about "dancing on the Milky Way." None of these other heavenly bodies, however, could match the brilliant comet. Father understood rain clouds, but he knew nothing about stars. Events that never affected the growing of his crops held very little interest for him.

An unusual bustle of people greeted us when we arrived at the square. They milled around waiting for the bus, but they were in no mood for conversation. Money-Roy waited too. He rarely left the square and often entertained himself by harassing people passing through.

As we waited in the dark, Mass Jim, Miss Mattie's husband, hopped in his truck with the spryness of a teenager. Normally, he maintained the mildest temperament of any man I knew. The man never raised his voice or yelled, as my father did. Now he bellowed, gunned the engine repeatedly, and blasted the horn to puncture the silence. Everyone glared in his direction, curious about his unusual haste.

Mass Jim owned a truck that supplied his family's shops in the neighboring districts. A shrewd businessman, he used Money-Roy to lift loads onto his truck. Money-Roy possessed brute strength in his burly frame.

Mass Jim tried to drag Father into a noisy argument about the government. Father stayed quiet. Lately, he rarely talked politics. All over the nation, people no longer debated in public, and instead killed each other over politics. Mr. Singer, the prime minister, had died suddenly, and a new leader joined Jamaican public discourse.

The new political leaders authorized clashes between gangs, making a mock of the *out of many one people* national slogan. People in the big city split into armed encampments trying to eradicate each other. A new term, *tribal war* entered the national psyche. City folks had electricity, but their lives were darker than my village on a moonless night.

City folks renamed their beautiful neighborhoods after international war zones. Kirkpatrick City became Dunkirk, Mountain View came to be called Waterloo, and Waterhouse turned into Firehouse. Our transistor radio on the cabinet at home broadcasted burning, looting, and killings in the city. I dreaded touching the transistor lest the violence flare up in our quiet mountain. Father and Mass Jim were on different sides of the political divide, but they were from the old days when men talked politics without bloodshed.

Ricky, my elementary school classmate, strolled from the back of the shop and pulled himself up next to his dad, Mass Jim. His father was taking him to a school in the plains. The man whipped the truck around and lined up for the ride to town. Abruptly, he stopped and motioned for me to join them in the cab. Neither he nor his wife, Miss Mattie, ever left me by the side of the road if I needed a ride. I jumped up to the running board of the truck. A free ride to school allowed me to save a bus fare. That money could buy lunch for a week.

I glanced back at Father standing at the crossroad, watching the vehicle carrying his son with a father's vision and the promise of an education. His hand gripped the machete's handle, blade at the ready. Suddenly, he spun around back to the fields he knew so well. Darkness swallowed him.

The truck's heavy door thudded shut. Mass Jim released the clutch, and I fell into the seat next to Ricky.

The man wheeled the truck around tight turns as if driving a car. I never guessed he possessed such fine driving skills. Normally he hardly spoke to anyone, but now he made eye contact and engaged me in a delightful chatter. To my surprise, he knew a lot about my family, and he complimented my father's intense work ethic.

I liked this new, energetic Mass Jim. If my father drove a truck, he would race it as Mass Jim now did.

Ricky sat next to me, silent and stone-faced. I knew him well enough to understand that fear gripped him. We shared the same bench during Mr. Beastly's reign of terror at the elementary school. Even then, Ricky always showed his emotions on his face.

In the cab, the ice between father and son grew by the minute. Mass Jim ignored Ricky as he sped down the winding road to town. The boy just fixed his gaze on the road as the headlights chased the darkness ahead of us.

Chapter 53

The trip to town took half the usual time. Mass Jim dropped me off at the side of the road, and I set out to walk the half a mile up to my classroom. Behind me, darkness wrapped the hills, and the comet still glared from the sky. I wondered if my father quarreled with Mamma before he left for the fields.

Mamma had trouble living with Father's hectic manner. A nervous atmosphere hung over our household from sunup to the dinner table. Father struck Mother on several occasions. One day, she packed a bag and left to work for a rich woman in the parish where she grew up. Everyone who left the valley always came back with money and better clothes. I expected that Mamma would soon start sending home letters filled with money.

We were useless without her. We helped Father cook our meals and tried to wash our clothes. The food tasted like starch and the clothes took too long to get clean. Two days later, Mamma returned, muttering she disliked cleaning the rich woman's floor, but I knew she'd missed us. I tried to balance the joy of having her back with the disappointment that she gave up on her freedom and happiness.

One Saturday, as I listened to my parents suffering through one of their irreconcilable disputes, I felt that I should try to end their sour saga. Next to me, a wooden stepladder leaned against the breadfruit tree. Tomorrow Father would use it to climb the breadfruit tree and harvest the fruits. With a long, weathered crack on one of the poles, the ladder seemed frail. I kicked at it, but it held firm. I smashed my boot repeatedly against the steps until it creaked and weakened. I left the ladder a wobbly mess. Anyone trying to climb the ladder would fall to certain death. I expected my father to be that person.

The next day, Father called me aside as always, and gave me my school allowance for the week, not a penny less. He paid for my education even as I set a trap for his demise.

At school the following Monday, I suffered thinking that I might have caused my father to fall from the ladder. *Did he use it to climb the breadfruit tree to pick fruits for dinner?* I went home, anxiously fearing the worst. As I passed through the crossroad, I glanced at Abbot. He would only speak to me if he brought bad news.

Father sat under the mango tree, resting after a day's work when I got home. I went to check on the ladder. It leaned where I left it. Father had neatly nailed a wooden slab over each of the cracks on the poles and made it good as new.

Relieved, I walked back to the kitchen. There I saw the breadfruits waiting to be cooked for my dinner. My dependency on Father grew clearer, even as I tried to accept my parents' unhappy union.

When the comet disappeared from our skies, Mass Jim resumed his mellow way of talking. Some of the worldlier citizenry explained that his odd behavior resulted from a dispute over a business deal gone sour. Slowly, everything returned to normal at the crossroad. Mass Jim's truck again climbed the hills at a snail's pace, and he resumed avoiding eye contact. Father continued his role as provider. Mother carried on watching her children's teeth set on edge as the father sucked the sour grapes. Abbot, the drunk, got that right.

Chapter 54

Father got on the minibus one morning to take the ride to school with me. He went to investigate why the school never sent home my scholarship money for books.

We walked together up the hill to the school. His gait slowed, and I paused so that he could catch up. By then, I had inherited his innate impatience and his talent for walking swiftly. Other students hurried past us as if we were oddities on the landscape. I hoped that Larry, the class gossip, would not ridicule us as we struggled up the hill. An aging parent made perfect fodder for Larry's mocking humor.

In one of my earliest memories of Father, he bursts around a corner of the road leading into our valley. He outpaces a jackass loaded down with produce from the fields. Most men might amble behind the donkey, carrying nothing but their own thoughts. Father bore a load enough for two men.

Across his shoulders, he carries a sack of yellow yams destined for our kitchen. In his right hand, he holds his machete, blade at the ready. Stride for stride, he races with the donkey. When the animal falters, his call fills the valley.

"Jack," and the hills echo "J-ack, J-ack, J-ack" back at him. The jackass skips a little to match his pace.

Together they race up the last hill to our house. Halfway up the hill, Father stops and unloads the produce. He waters the donkey and sets him free to forage. Father brings home food for everyone. He carries enough corn for the pigs, the chickens, and the milking cow. He supplied our kitchen very well.

As he labors up the hill leading up to the school, I had no patience with his halting steps. My book bag held pounds of books, so I could not help him with the bag of avocados that he brought for the principal. They were the finest fruits from our property, and he thought nothing of giving these good gifts to a woman who held up my scholarship money.

He hid his softer side from most people. I recalled an instant when he asked me to climb tangerine trees to pick fruits for the woman to take to the market. That late in the season, the fruits were scarce, and they fetched a good price in town. More tangerines meant more money for Christmas shopping. I wanted to find as many as I could. Father waited on the ground beneath the tree. He stood ready to catch the fruits with "soft hands" to avoid squashing them.

Every fruit I grabbed had a hole. Birds pierced holes through the fruits, pecked the insides clean, and left behind a hollowed cup. I cursed the birds for their overindulgence. From the ground, my father's voice came with surprising calm.

"Every mouth must be fed. Come down."

I never knew he cared about birds. He must be getting soft in his old age.

Stories about my father were fodder for folklore. A man named Val visited from the USA and told a tale of his experience with Father. Val was a household name for us because Father brought him up like a son. He frequently wrote to my dad from his home in Connecticut. Val's letters always contained gifts of money for Father, whom he fondly called Uncle.

Val's pop died decades before I was born. Father assumed the role of teaching the young Val about life.

Life meant hard work for my father. Val needed to provide for his widowed mom, and Father taught him how to grow food. Before dawn, they got ready to go to the fields. Father saddled the donkey and told Val to mount up on the packsaddle. The lad responded too slowly, and Father's shout shook the morning awake. Val sprang for the donkey's packsaddle and missed. In a panic, he had jumped over the animal clear to the other side.

When I saw Val for the first time, he bore no resemblance to the boy in the story. Time had taken his leap and his shoulders slumped a little. He and my father were now aging men, reliving the distant past.

The walk up to the school became the longest walk of my life. My father stopped again, and I felt like walking ahead. Back home in the hills, I always waited quietly while Father rested. I controlled my youthful zest to burst ahead. We were partners when on the road.

When he fought with Mamma, Father quietly tried to tell me his side of the conflict. In my heart, I knew that he did wrong, but never told him so. In her own time, Mamma told me her account. I always sided with her. I knew I could never be hard and offensive like Father.

For the first time, I walked away from my father. I left him behind puffing for air, the man who took me over this same route on my first day of school. I kept looking back and feeling that I made a worthless choice. I killed my albatross, and it hung heavily around my neck.

I glanced back to see if he was okay. He had edged forward clutching the bag of avocados clutched under his arm. I was not surprised. His fortitude was as real as legendary. If I had not been so schooled at suppressing my feelings, I would have cried in shame.

Chapter 55

A pretty girl from the business class in town arrived late to class again. I never found the courage to tell her that I liked the way her lips pouted before she smiled. Her family owned an auto parts store. My father owned a donkey. A huge social gap ran between us.

Tiptoeing, she danced to her seat and tentatively lifted the lid to place her books inside the desk. Her face froze in horror. As she gripped the lid, her desperate eyes swept the classroom pleading for help. She looked past the loudmouths, my studious classmates, and turned to me. She whimpered.

"Manny, there is a scorpion in my desk. Can you kill it for me?"

I sprang to my feet, thinking she was brave. Most would have screamed. She motioned me over and pointed inside of her desk. On the bottom of the desk and daring me to stick my hand inside, a black scorpion poised menacingly. I stared at the creature from my nightmares. The beast held its tail high, torqueing it defiantly.

In an instant, all that I knew about scorpions flashed through my mind. They struck faster than lightning. Death and infirmity lay waiting in their stingers. They were quick and could switch direction to strike. Scorpions can compress themselves, slip in a crevice, and vanish.

Did it follow me here? I thought they infested old haunts like our home back in the hills. Everything was brand new in this classroom.

In one deft move, I flipped the desk upside-down to eject the scorpion. The creature landed on the concrete floor and shot toward my feet. I raised my leg and stomped. I swore I got him, but I saw no sign of the kill. He had disappeared.

A long moment, and the fears scorpions represented, shivered through me. I became Father in the latrine, sitting on the wooden toilet seat as the scorpion pierced my arse in the dark hour before dawn. I shivered as the venom spread through my body.

From my years at the elementary school, I recalled Mr. Beastly's Scorpion belt piercing my back. Electric shocks from the lightning striking me in the post office stung my legs. I burned with the shame of wearing the label *backward man from the Mocho Mountain.* I smelled defeat on the rum-laced belches of men at the crossroad bar, even my own fear.

The girl fired a quizzical look at me, perhaps thinking she picked the wrong person. Caught in the tension of beauty and the beast, I kept my eyes on the scorpion. I was the man for this job.

I knew where the beast hid waiting. He had slipped into the space between the heel and the sole of my shoe and was ready to dart up my leg and inject his poison into my arse. I raised my heel and slammed my foot on the hard floor again. Guts and ooze splashed across the room forming perfect lines in the cardinal directions. When I lifted my shoes, what remained of its armor-plated exoskeleton sat at the intersection of its innards, a ghost at the crossroad.

The girl exhaled and mumbled her thanks. She slipped into her seat and I slipped into mine. The mathematics teacher never once stopped his lesson to recognize that I just crushed my childhood nightmare.

Next day, the lines of scorpion guts were still there. The normally diligent custodian failed to sweep them away. In time, the lines faded, along with my fear of the black scorpion.

Chapter 56

The bus conductor pointed to the space designated for children—a board spanning the aisles. I elbowed my way to the back of the packed bus and squeezed into the seat. As a sixteen-year-old, I was lucky to ride this bus to the best high school in town.

"School boy, git up. Seat's feh full-price customer."

For years, the voice of the ill-tempered bus conductor kept reminding me that schoolchildren only paid a half fare. His family owned everything of value back home in the village. He knew how to wield that power. I relinquished my seat and stretched across the back of the seat like a lizard on a limb. A half-price bus fare provided my pass to the halls of learning. If they'd charged me a full fare, I would never have gone to school.

Long days in transit to school forced me to adapt quickly. I shoved the fare at the conductor before he could ask for it. Accurate to the penny, it appeased the man. He nodded, grasped the money, and twitched impatiently at the woman in the next seat. She fumbled in a thread bag tucked away in her bosom and fished out a few crumpled dollars. I looked away. We were almost home.

Swirls of red dust chased the minibus as we labored home. A few meager clouds in the sky offered scant relief from the heat. Trees sat motionless in the sun. The powdery taste of dirt seeped into the bus. It smelled like home.

The bus whipped past a tall, athletic figure running on the road. I recognized my friend, Will, the only soul to jog this six-mile stretch from Cedars to the village. His face stared at the road, unmoved. He was the finest athlete the community had ever produced.

"Sports changed my life."

Will previously confessed that he used his athletic experiences to escape his backward country upbringing. A year earlier he'd graduated from high school in town, and now he led the local church youth group. Will taught at the secondary school while he saved money to attend university in the big city.

As the bus bounced home, I yearned to be like my confident friend. He raised himself above local superstition and folks never tried to tell him how to run his life. Most people just let him be, as if he was above reproach.

The bus stopped at the square. I got off and waited for him to come running up. Out of earshot of others, I inquired timidly, "Will, can I run with you from Cedars?"

"Mmhmm," he agreed.

He expressed no reservation, although I doubted my stamina.

Next day, after school, I got off the bus at Cedars. I felt unsure about the run, but my heart told me to try. I stooped to lace up my running shoes, hoping that the drunks at the bar would distract the students away from me. Will towered over me, waiting.

A man stumbled out of the rum bar, squinting at the light. He sized us up. Unimpressed, he spat and retreated to the shadows. Some men could drink the afternoon away.

"You are goin' to jog with him?" a voice in the crowd snorted and gestured toward Will. Everyone admired my friend's legendary stamina. I gulped fear and nodded.

"He is goin' to pull out you tripe on Guinea Corn Hill," the cynic heckled.

The crowd chuckled in agreement. A torment of steep slopes ran up Guinea Corn Hill. Vehicles stalled as they tried to scale the inclines.

The heckler knew nothing about running, but I knew the local beliefs that backed him up.

"If you run in the hot sun, you will drop down by the roadside."

I avoided the doubter's glare. Good advice was as scarce as pocket money. Without ceremony, Will led off. His feet barely brushed the loose pebbles on the road. I followed tentatively.

We ran easily over the gentle rolling landscape of the first mile, but Guinea Corn Hill loomed. We trotted past a broken-down BMC minivan. It perched by the side of the hill, rusted through, and filled with defeat. BMC vans were always overheating and falling apart on our steep hillsides.

Halfway up the hill, the ill advice of the cynical boy boiled up and tightened my guts. The afternoon sun beat down and created mirages in the dips in the road ahead. A wave of nausea spread from my gut, cramping my legs.

Doubts swarmed through my head. *Mamma often warned me never to exert my frail body. There were no runners in my family. What about the seer who threatened to make me walk and pick up rubbish, like the village crazy man?* I could go no farther.

I begged Will to stop so I could catch my breath, but my friend would not let me fail. Instead, he reached back and offered his hand. I sprinted to catch up. Will ran faster. I grasped at the hand, but I could not catch up. This game got us over the hill.

At the crest, the relief I felt from the climb ending almost brought tears to my eyes. I had challenged the myth of Guinea Corn Hill and won. As I pressed on, the toil became more about my will to run and less about my untrained legs.

My thighs throbbed just as hard running down the other side of the hill. Will's bulging muscles kept pumping ahead of me. I gritted my teeth and trudged along. Four miles of hills and gullies lay ahead.

Every bone ached. My heart said quit, I'd run enough for one day. I wanted to drop by the side of the road when we passed a group of girls walking home. Failing to see my faltering heart, they cheered. I straightened up and showed off my best strides. The girls clapped louder. I ran harder.

Two miles from the square, the first drops ushered in an afternoon downpour. The road quickly emptied. Folks fled for shelter lest they catch a cold. With only the sound of our feet sloshing on the path, we ran into the downpour.

On the vacant road, I ran my fastest mile. The rain became my new friend, bathing me with confidence. My legs grew stronger with each step. The moist air took me back to the smell of fresh laundry flapping on the clothesline at home.

We approached the village cemetery with the belfry towering above the Anglican Church. Now and then, the bell's toll signaled the passing of a local soul. My older sister lay buried among the neighborhood dead.

Sensing my qualms, Will broke his silence.
"Come."

I fled past the ghosts of the valley waiting for me to "drop down" and join them in their silent tombs. I raced until I heard his steady breathing.

The final peak before we broke into the square was the most formidable. It ascended quickly and twisted off into the fog. Fittingly named School Hill, the slope ran past Principal Beastly's elementary school. Local lore celebrated its steepness with the tale of Braman, the Rasta man rolling an empty fifty-five-gallon drum up the hill.

I recalled my elementary school classmates taunting the Rasta man. Braman pushed the drum two steps up, and the hill rolled him back down two. He shoved again, and the steep incline drove him back. The older boys teased and sang a ska tune about a man who would never die, a "hard man fe dead." The last I saw of the incident was Braman's legs stuck in the opening as the drum rolled him downhill.

As I took my turn on School Hill, I faced my "good for nothing" feeling and fought the fear of failing. Wet sneakers skidded on the road, and I reached for my friend's hand. I lowered my head to avoid seeing the sheer enormity of the climb. Slowly I ran past the memory of my cousin, Braman, rolling backward down the slope. Inch by inch, I passed the school where the headmaster had beaten me into submission.

Deep inside a warm feeling began to spread across my stomach. The warmth stifled the fear that I was too weak to be a runner. I sped past the spot where lightning killed the tall mahoe tree and scarred the patchy asphalt road. I ran out of the shackles of the old myth that my "heart-string would bust" from exertion. Loads lifted from my shoulders.

Behind me, I knew, mountains stacked behind the other mountains that framed my ascent. I had climbed them all. I never looked back. Ahead even higher mountains loomed, but I would not climb up any more mountains today.

I dropped my eyes to the ground and scrambled up to Will. We sprinted down the other side of the hill past Braman's house. The fifty-five-gallon drum sat in his yard. The Rasta man, too, had defeated School Hill and brought home the drum to collect rainwater for his kitchen. His chant came from behind the house.

Someday, someday … The song hoped for better days.

Shoulder to shoulder, Will and I ran into the square. Rain washed us over. I basked in its cleansing power.

There were a few idlers mixed in with folks sheltering from the downpour at the crossroad shop. Many heads turned to stare at us racing over hills and gullies. We were defying myths instead of turning our hands to the plough as our fathers. Not a soul applauded.

The resident drunk, Abbot, stared intently, probing for a sign of weakness. I avoided him. His eyes knew too much.

Chapter 57

Confident with my emerging athletic prowess, I formed a soccer team to play a match with youths from the neighboring community. Everyone played cricket, lovely cricket, but no one played soccer in our valley. I turned to my friend Will to help me train our team. We introduced cricketers to the fine art of dribbling and shooting at a soccer goal.

By now, Will and I knew how to organize community events. We had different yet complimentary leadership styles. He led with his bold, positive approach, and I made sure everyone had fun participating. We were used to singing in the choir and putting on plays for the church congregation. Our youth choir won several awards at national church conventions.

Fifteen lads responded to our call to join the soccer team. The young man who volunteered to be the goalkeeper surprised us all. Goal keeping is the most specialized position on the team, and the skill take years to acquire.

When we placed our young man between the makeshift goalposts, he pounced on every ball with the instinct of a cat. We had our man. Our team practiced and planned for Mikey, the captain of the squad from the next village.

Will and I anchored the midfield, switching between offense and defense. I acquired the reputation of being fast on my feet from people who saw me running with Will. We were undoubtedly the fittest duo between the two teams.

The teams walked the six miles to Cedars to face off on the soccer field. Our players reflected a slice of our community. In the crude mixture were a storekeeper, aspiring farmers, students, the unemployed, and a teacher.

On game day, some wore pus-crepe shoes, but most were barefooted. My younger brother Serge and I owned soccer cleats that my older brother had given us. Will brought out cleats from his high school days.

I knew all the boys on the other team. At one time or the other, we sat in Mr. Beastly's little school when they called us cutthroats from Killman Park. Back then, Mikey, their leader, sat behind me in the principal's class. Before the game, we chatted with relief about surviving Mr. Beastly's torment.

During the game, Will and I played the midfield link so we could set up the offense or preempt any attempts to test our new goalkeeper's skill. Few balls got past us. We lived up to our reputation of fitness and speed. Will and I set up many opportunities for our forwards to score, but they missed with wild shots on goal.

We won on a penalty shot as our frustrated opponents lashed out because of their inability to control the ball. No one bragged about the score. Everyone seemed to recognize that we made history by playing the first soccer match between the two villages that feared each other because of the murders at the crossroad.

Chapter 58

Shadows from an afternoon shower softened the hard edges off the land. Rain washed the smell of red dust from the air, and life again sprang from our parched hillsides. Pale, limp leaves on the citrus trees turned lush after a drink from the damp soil.

The long dry season ended, and our water tanks quickly filled up with the precious fluid. As the downpour ended, the evening sun brushed away every piece of cloud and touched the hills with a haze of gold.

In a light and easy mood, I got on the minibus with Will. The van navigated the hills, and the passengers sank into a blissful silence as we headed home. We were rural folks mulling over the daily routine of chopping wood, cooking at the fire, and planting more corn. *Will I get home by dusk to bring home the goats before nightfall?*

At Cedars, the junction before we switched on to the back roads, a girl quietly boarded the bus. She seemed about seventeen, my age. Her unblemished skin, city clothes, and the buoyant energy flowing from her ponytail said that she was not regular country folk. She flitted to the empty seat in front of me, and I fought hard the temptation to reach out and touch her. She brought the smell of jasmine, perfumed baths, and the elegant lifestyles of faraway places.

"I know you. You are 'Night Medic'."

The girl's voice broke the reverie like a solitary drop of water falling into a crystalline pool and tinkling into the air. She turned to look at Will. My older, athletic friend often got the attention from the girls. Before he responded, I seized the moment and probed.

"You know Will? He's got a nickname?"

Without hesitation, she let me ease into her conversation. She explained that a year ago, she was a junior in the same school that Will attended on the other side of town. My friend was an excellent student during the day, but one night they caught him sneaking into the girls' dormitory. The girls called him "Night Medic," a secretive prowler with an innocent charm.

Will appeared uncomfortable with the nickname. He sometimes preached at the local church, and people looked up to him. In our village, nobody knew him as the Night Medic.

He remained aloof to the excitement that filled the air when the girl spoke. He turned his head and stared at the vegetation outside the window. I reached forward in the seat stealing more of the magic resonance as the girl talked. I made up chatter just to hear her voice.

For the first time, the ride on the bus ended too quickly. The air emptied as she departed. I fixated on her crossing the lawn to a tiny cottage and ached after the bounce in her ponytail. She ignored the faces pressed against the glass, watching the late evening sun touching her so lightly. I wished I knew her name.

The stoic Rastafarian driving the Toyota minibus stared and salivated too. He enjoyed the reputation of moving on any girl who rode in his van. A wife and a couple of babies at home failed to stop him from fathering other *picaninny* outside his marriage. This was not his kind of girl. She was better than both of us.

Skillfully, he pulled the van from the curb and fingered the steering wheel through the treacherous turns across the hills. The huge hat on his head, stuffed with long dreadlocks, did not bob in the slightest. His eyes watched me in the rearview mirror, sizing me up. While he drove, the locks remained as obscured and forbidden as his dour mood.

When we got to the square, he removed his hat, and his locks uncoiled and tumbled to his waist. He smiled, apparently relieved from the job of driving his father's van all day. His father led the congregation in songs at my church. Father and son were on opposite sides of the religious divide.

I paused at the square to prod Will about the girl's name.

"Singh," he replied boringly. "I don't know her first name. Her family owns the biggest business in town."

I could not understand why Will failed to sense the excitement from the pretty butterfly who'd just touched our lives. I would probably never see her again. It was the last weekend of summer, and, on Monday, I would be back on the daily commute for my final year in high school.

Chapter 59

I felt ambivalent about returning to school because I had already earned enough credits to graduate. Would my aging father be able to support me for two more years in the Advanced Level program? Since I could not find a job, I decided to sign up for the Advanced Level curriculum. Later, I planned to apply to the university in the big city. Most of my colleagues in the Advanced Level program were ardent scholars. I never studied as I should, but I got away with it often enough.

The atmosphere in the Advanced Level classes was more relaxed than the lower classes. We could miss class without any consequences other than missing coursework for an exam. I could always read the book. The teachers were friendlier too. Some of them were merely a few years older than I and were not opposed to a flirtatious compliment.

My closest friends, Longers and Josie, were excellent students, but they were open to testing some of the routines at school. Longers could read an entire book as he walked to school. Josie's quiet, easygoing manner contrasted with the other boys in town. He kept his thoughts to himself.

We sneaked off campus and hiked to the sugarcane plantation three miles away. Josie led us for a swim in the clear waters of the irrigation canals. Afterward, we snatched a few sugarcane stems from the nearby plantation.

Without a care in the world, we ambled back to school, ripping the skin off the sugarcane to suck the sweet juice in the stem. On the way, a Ford Transit minibus loaded with passengers from the big city, Kingston, hustled past us. The name *Sweet Jamaica* blazed from the back of the fleeting bus. Josie dropped his piece of sugarcane and gaped after the vehicle.

"My mamma packed us in that same van, and we fled tribal war in Kingston," he confided.

He gave a glimpse of his life as a boy-soldier in the city where gun-toting political gangs fought each other.

"Sometimes I was up all-night firing till the gun mouth run red hot."

"Shooting at what?" Longers prodded.

"Everyone afraid of each other. Shooting so the next political gang won't come kill us while we sleep."

"You kill anybody?" I joined. He paused and dropped his eyes to the ground.

"You're too inquisitive but hear this. I remember a white wall with the words scrawled in red paint, 'Jamaica-land of wood and water now turned murder and manslaughter'."

He clamped shut his lips and refused to say another word. We slipped back into class and pretended we never left. At the end of the day, I hurried to catch the big country bus home.

I hopped up the steps of the bus and saw a girl looking for a seat. She was a picture of neatness with an Afro groomed with delicate flicks of her pick. Her unblemished skin captured the smoothness of a deep pond untouched by light or ruffled by wind. She looked me over with big eyes that showed the faintest beginnings of a smile.

From the color of her school's uniform, I knew she attended the secretarial academy in town. She folded every pleat on her skirt and carefully sat down. Even at the end of the day, her clothes were crisp and flawless.

Normally, I spend a quarter of the daylight hours traveling back and forth to school in the plains. In the morning, I took the faster minivan to get to school. In the evening, I boarded the country bus for the sluggish ride home. The other passengers napped. I could use a lively conversation en-route home.

The girl's white blouse stretched tight across her chest in the full flush of womanhood. I let my eyes probe beyond the fabric to the dark contours beneath. I could not resist the empty seat next to her.

She glanced at me and then resumed staring forward. I peeked at her profile and watched the light disappear into her jet-black hair. After I introduced myself, we chatted easily. We babbled throughout the afternoon as the bus left the town behind and climbed the winding road up the mountain.

Her name was Virginia, but she preferred Gina. As the bus rounded the curves, our shoulders touched, and we stayed that way for the rest of the ride. When we got to her stop, I strutted down the steps with her book bag and waited for her at the bottom of the rung. She descended with flair, her uniform a royal gown, and with equal gallantry, I handed her the bag. The smile she flashed lit up the evening air. Over my shoulder, I saw faces peering longingly from the windows. The bus driver smiled patiently as I climbed back onboard to my seat.

After school the next day, I hustled eagerly to the bus stop to see Gina. Her book bag sat on the seat next to her, saving it for me. She lifted it up and placed it on the floor. We forgot about the stench of the sweaty passengers and the pungent belch from the tail pipe as the bus burned diesel fuel and climbed the hills.

Gina came from the parish of Saint Mary in the east side of the island. There, prevailing winds from the ocean brought rainfall almost every day. She'd moved to live with her brother in a district barely a mile from my home.

This became our daily routine. Her school was closer to the bus stop, so she claimed the best seat and guarded my place next to where she spread her skirt. Soon enough, the other passengers learned to keep away from my seat. I helped her off the bus when she got to her stop.

I had never been this close to a woman who seemed ready to draw me into her sensuous world. I desperately wanted to make an impression, so I decided to use my best tool to get beyond the casual talk. I wrote a poem in praise of her beauty.

I held her hands and read the poem. She touched the calluses that I earned from swinging the axe to chop firewood on weekends. A smile played on her lips as she listened. Abruptly she dropped my hand.

Just as quickly, she picked it up again. A slow glow spread over her face. We rode the rest of the trip like that, quietly clutching hands and feeling the details on each other's fingers. The country bus bounced over the rough road, and we held on and ignored the red dirt that stained the floors.

The next day, Gina's smile welcomed me onto the bus. She pressed a small brown envelope in my hand as I sat down. I opened the letter she penned in response to my poem. She wrote that the poems thrilled her, and she promised to tell me more on the ride home.

"Be your best self, and stay cool, but never forget God, your first love," she wrote.

We never talked about religion, and her ending caught me off guard. Outside of my community, I kept secret my very active role in the local church. At school, I wore an amorphous face as I tried to blend away the traces of my country roots. When I left home for school, I left behind church, goat rearing, and the rural lifestyle.

Perhaps Gina's faith helped to maintain the cool that I so admired. As a closet Christian, my faith never followed me as closely. Soon, we resumed our chatter and forgot about poetry or piety.

When we got to her stop, I walked her down the steps. Earlier, afternoon showers washed the heat away from the hills. Runoff percolating through the soil changed the relentless red dirt to a tamer brown. The soft light of the approaching evening filtered through the few clouds remaining, and it gently flowed over her skin. Her face glowed. We paused staring at each other, lost in the sweet innocence that passes too quickly.

The bus driver let us stand there a minute longer than usual. Unlike the Rasta man who drove the minivan, he never leered at the schoolgirls. The diesel engine roared to life as he teased the accelerator. I leapt to the door and hopped onto the moving vehicle.

The moment lingered for the rest of the ride. When I got to my stop, the driver slowed down, and light on my feet, I skipped off and ran all the way up to my house.

Chapter 60

In class, everyone talked about a "new girl" who just transferred to our school. The boys babbled about her popularity, money, or her beauty. Her family had just built the tallest building in town. She seemed like local royalty. I paid scant attention to the gossip. Gina waited for me, holding my seat for a sweet bus ride over the mountains.

As I walked to class a few weeks later, I saw the Singh girl, whom I'd met on the bus earlier that summer. I did not expect to see her here, decked out in our school's maroon tunic uniform. So, this is the "new girl" in school? Only now, she let her hair down, toppling halfway down her face.

She sat under a tree with branches cascading halfway to the ground and held court with a bunch of her girls. Nearby, a few boys vied for her attention. I walked up to her and said hello. She left her company of friends, and we broke into fist of chitchatting and smiling. She kept looking up at me as if she could see something special in my eyes. No girl ever stared at me like that.

She told me that when I saw her in the summer, she was visiting her grandmother. Her girlfriends looked daggers at me for interrupting. The boys lying in wait shuffled uncomfortably and cursed at the intruding Mocho Manny. Disregarding their hostility, we talked, and her eyes twinkled.

"What's your name?"

"Jasmine. It means fragrance."

In my heart, I already knew what her name meant. I still remembered her scent from the previous summer.

The next day I made sure I ran into her again. As an upper-class student, I monitored the class next to hers, keeping the students quiet until the teacher arrived. I found her easily. Again, she had a following, but she instantly broke away and glided toward me. We chatted, forgetting that we were at school. The bell rang, and we stopped staring into each other's eyes.

Jasmine reached inside her tunic and pulled a letter from inside her bosom. She moved a little bit closer, and I smelled her fragrance, soft and tantalizing. She touched the note gently against my chest.

"Can you give this to Ma Rene?" she asked. Her eyes held the smallest glint of gold as she watched at me. I nodded, knowing that she asked me to stop at her grandma's on my way home to deliver her letter. She whirled and walked quickly to the friends glaring in my direction.

I glanced at the neat writing on the letter, and I wondered why she made a fuss over an ol' woman. The grumpy minibus driver never made unscheduled stops to drop off notes. I would be walking across Ma Rene's lawn before a minivan filled with villagers.

A faint trace of perfume drifted up to my nose, and I brought the letter closer. I imagined the tenderness where it nestled before she gave it to me. I stuck the letter in my breast pocket. It dropped out of sight, and I visualized it there, all pink and full of warmth. I wished I knew the name of that perfume.

I let the country bus leave without me because I did not want Gina to see me getting off the bus and delivering the perfumed letter. Later, I got on the same minivan on which I met Jasmine earlier that summer. The minivan ran its last trip late in the evening.

I thought twice about asking the dreadlocked driver to stop and wait for me while I delivered the letter. His surly mood ran like a barrier between him and the male passengers since he never did favors for men. However, this was the last ride home, and if I missed this van, I would have to walk three miles from the nearest village to get home.

"Could you hold a minute while I drop off something for Ma Rene?" I asked. I expected him to growl a negative answer, and I was prepared to get off and walk home if he refused to wait. Without acknowledging that I'd spoken, he stopped the van.

I jumped out and fled across the lawn. I could feel his eyes burning in my back, straining to uncover the insides of the envelope that I carried so daintily. One knock on the door and Ma Rene opened it.

"Jasmine asked me to give you this letter," I blurted.

The woman's smile lit her eyes. She fiddled with the envelope, trying to decipher its contents. In a few minutes, I ran back to the minivan. The driver sat impatiently, and, in the quiet before he drove off, he gave the longest speech I ever heard him make. Without turning, he growled from the side of his face.

"You must be careful not to make that girl turn you into a messenger bwoy."

How did he know that girl gave me a note? I never told him. His voice resounded scornfully with the insincere advice of a rival. In all the years that I rode his van, he never spoke to me. After a long pause, he turned to watch my reaction. A long piece of dreadlock snaked out from beneath his hat and flicked like the tail of the scorpion that had stung my father.

I held my tongue. His powerful family controlled most of our community. They owned the largest grocery stores, the gas station, and the buses that took me to school daily. I knew how to walk around people and their inflated egos and still get my business done.

Faint traces of perfume remained on my shirt where the letter had nestled close to my heart. This letter carried the sweetest message I'd ever held, and I would be delighted to carry many more. This girl was too good for the bearded man.

The next day I went to see Jasmine on the pretense that I delivered her note. She seemed more interested in talking and staring up into my eyes. We stood so close that I smelled that perfume again. By then, the rumormongers were claiming she was my girlfriend, and I needed to know how she felt about me, so I plucked up the courage and asked the question.

"Jasmine, the whole school is saying you are my girlfriend, will you like to become my gir...?"

My voice trailed off as I waited for the long explanation about her family and their elevated standing and my backward boy from Mocho status. My chest heaved a little as I waited. She moved closer and her eyes locked with mine.

"Yes," she said, as if it were the most natural thing in the world.

I took a couple of deep breaths and calmed myself. In the back of my mind, I felt that I just turned a page on the innocent years. The august buildings on the school campus seemed warmer and friendlier. As I walked back to my class, my feet barely touched ground and I couldn't get the idiotic smile off my face.

That evening after school, Jasmine and I strolled to town where her parents ran their business. It became the longest walk of my life. I tried to stall so that by the time I arrived in town, the country bus would be halfway up the mountain with Gina. I did not want her to see me with Jasmine.

Time slowed to long ticks of a clock about to go out of wind. Arm in arm, we rounded a corner and ran into the parked bus collecting its last passenger before it angled up the mountain. The bus, too, ran on a slowed clock. I dropped Jasmine's hand, but she reached for my hand with the pull of a magnet.

I tried not to look at the bus where Gina sat in her favorite seat with my place reserved next to her. She sat straining through the dusty window to see me. She knew the route that I usually walked from school to meet her. She smiled in anticipation as she glimpsed me. Then she saw Jasmine walking next to me, holding my hand with bold possessiveness. Gina froze, then sat bolt upright in her seat. Her face twisted in shock and pain. Slowly she turned her head to look forward, calm and composed like the first time I met her. Jasmine wound her fingers around mine tighter.

The bus delayed, conspiring to prolong this painful encounter. It stalled for long minutes as the burly conductor tossed the market women's empty containers up to the luggage rack. I held Jasmine's hand as we passed under the window where Gina and I spent many afternoons sharing the long ride home. Arm in arm, we stepped past the bus full of the same people who daily watched me sitting close to Virginia's pleated skirts.

The seat that she reserved for me remained empty. She turned away from me, and we did not acknowledge each other. From the corner of my eyes, I glimpsed her profile. Her eyes were distant as the cool hills of her parish, Saint Mary. I did not know how to say that someone else had stolen my heart.

Chapter 61

School became a way to pass time as I waited to see Jasmine. We spent every second of the midmorning break talking. Mostly, we were there for the sparks that flew between us. Other suitors waited, her girlfriends wanted every minute of her time, but she walked away to be with me. I spent lunchtime with my friend Longers, praying for dismissal so I could walk to town with Jasmine at my side.

One afternoon it began to rain as we started the walk to town. Everyone ran for shelter, but Jasmine pulled a pink umbrella from her bag and motioned for me to join her under the warm glow of the umbrella. I wrapped my arm around her waist as we walked, and I hugged her for the first time. Her soft curves moved under my hand as we strolled.

The rain tapered to a drizzle, but we stayed under the umbrella. We passed a woman barely older than us, and she scoffed at Jasmine and said something uncomplimentary about her legs. I wrapped my arms about her protectively. She snuggled closer. We walked past the unflattering woman and disregarded her attempt to change the atmosphere under the pretty pink umbrella.

Far too soon, we were at her parents' store. I could not go near their place of business. Her mom ran the store, and boys were not permitted to talk to her daughter. Jasmine warned that we must keep our romance a secret. We pulled apart, sensing the gloom of the rain clouds for the first time. I watched the umbrella speed off with her and cheered myself with the thought that tomorrow I would be king when I saw her again.

I hurried on to catch the bus home, since the distant hills too were black with rain clouds. The fickle bus driver cut his workday short because it rained too much. I took another bus that stopped short of the village square and then walked the miles through Foga woods to get home.

The quiet hills gave me the setting to write poetry about my newfound love. I stayed up late at night nursing the lamplight until I finished. The next day I read the poem as I held Jasmine's hand. She sat there somewhat awed, as if I'd said something magical. I felt like I was the only person in the world.

My friends noticed my tardiness to class. They openly speculated, "What this wealthy girl want with the Mocho man?" One morning, Jasmine arrived at school later than usual, and she came straight to my class. She beckoned for me to meet her outside the door. She held my hand briefly and gave me a bar of chocolate. Quietly, she looked up at me with soft eyes, and I forgot that I was the Mocho man.

I shared the chocolate with Josie and Longers, my two friends. The delicious chocolate sent a powerful message. Mocho Manny had won over the heart of the most sought-after girl in school. After Longers finished snacking, he chuckled and gave me warning.

"We are going to laugh at you when that girl leaves you, Manny."

Longers was my best ally at school, got in a fight with Larry the bully on my behalf. My friend still bore the scars from Larry's blows. He only meant that I should proceed with caution with the "new girl." I was reaching above my status to mingle with a girl from the upper class. I dismissed him, thinking about the poem I wrote for Jasmine. At break time, I read it to her.

Unending

And she planted a rose
of beauty and fragrance unknown
in a garden of flesh.
Another came disguised
to steal the rose
yet it blossomed a sweet bouquet
and a vision of love.

Chapter 62

"I am coming to Mocho tonight to visit my grandmother," Jasmine chirped, her eyes filled with a promise. I could not wait to visit her in the secrecy of the Mocho Mountains. I got on the last bus from the plains to arrive at dusk. Light as a feather, I walked the mile from the bus stop to her grandmother's place.

Brown dusk slipped into night as I arrived at the house. Not a soul could see my approach. Her mother planted spies everywhere to report on her activities. Moreover, I attracted a lot of negative attention from just about everyone who wanted Jasmine's attention.

I knocked at the door softly. Like an instant echo, it sprang open. Jasmine closed it softly behind her and sprang into my arms. I embraced her tiny waist, pulled her face upward, and pressed her lips for the first kiss. It was all that I expected, warm, soft, probing, responding, and melting. We needed no words. All that staring into each other's eyes down in the plains peaked in a moment.

I reached for her bosom to find the source of the perfume that always touched her letters. Everything was soft and smooth, like the flow of honey. Fragrance, flesh, texture, and breath rolled into one flurry of sensation.

No sound came from inside the little house. The night blanketed us away from the neighborhood, and time stopped. When we were tired of squeezing each other, we walked slowly to the back of the house and leaned against a koala nut tree and hug hugged some more. She had chosen a perfect night with only the stars to bear witness. We needed no light. We lit our own flame. When I could find the voice to speak, I asked about her perfume that obsessed my dreams.

"Rose-apple bloom," she said, as if it were the most natural thing in the world. I pulled her close again and buried my face where rose-apple bloom mixed with feminine flower.

Later on, that night, the moon peered over the hills to the east. In the moonlight, I saw her more clearly. Her hair, unrestrained, fell past her face, with the wavy ends flicking upward before touching her shoulders. We leaned on the tree, trusting the shadowed canopy to keep our secrets.

On her grandmother's third call, we gave one final kiss and split apart for the night. I bounced along the rocky road with my feet in the clouds. I saw nobody on the way. Except for someone seeking the embrace of a new love, most country folks went to bed at dusk. Warmed to the heart, I refused dinner at home. I barely slept.

The moon rose earlier the next night, and Jasmine and I sat down on a concrete ledge under the kola nut tree that sheltered us the previous night. I had never seen a prettier night in these hills. Moonlight lit every peak and chased the shadows from under each bush. The whole village fell quiet except for our hushed voices.

"I have a secret flaw to show you," she whispered. She pulled back her hair and leaned toward me.

"One of my ears is deformed, pointy. Got it from my father's family.

I saw nothing.

"You are flawless."

I did not tell her about my flaw, my fear of becoming a wife-beater like Father. We talked into the night. Sometimes we stopped and listened to the passing of time. Nothing stirred around us.

Ma Rene called for Jasmine to come inside earlier than usual. Her normally cheerful voice seemed filled with strain and disapproval. We leaned against a tree for a long, parting kiss. The tree swayed gently. A change in the wind ruffled the tops of the trees. She shuddered a little and I wrapped her in my arms as long as I could.

Oh Tree

I hear you distinctly,
echoing hushed words of love
in your windblown voice.
I feel cool

beneath your spreading branches
that frees us to love.
I lean against you
safe from peering eyes,
You are strong,
bearing both our bodies

Chapter 63

I lived a dual existence between school and my home in the hills. During the week, I rode the bus to town where I sat with the children of the leading citizens. At the end of the day and on weekends, I again lived the parochial life. I slipped back and forth between the two different societies with ease.

At school, my friends never asked about my life in the hills. They were probably already in bed while I trudged home waiting for the bus that never came, or I'd stayed too long talking to Jasmine after school. Often, I walked the last five miles in the dark to my house because no bus ran back to our village after brown dusk. The next day, I stumbled through explaining why I did not complete my homework. I could not let on that I fell asleep reading by the dim light of a kerosene lamp. I could never admit I lived in a backward village with no electricity.

On weekends, I still spent time with Sonny. When I attended school in town, he went on to the same local secondary school that Angie attended. Sonny's household had changed. His dad, Isaiah, lost the tight grip on their property. One by one his children ran away to escape the stigma of their incestuous lineage.

Soon only Sonny and his older brother Curly remained. While their dad was stingy, Sonny and Curly gave away Isaiah's wealth. When our oranges ran out for the season, we got some of Isaiah's sugary Valencia oranges. Sonny stole his dad's money and gave it away to needy people. Isaiah could not stop the sway of the pendulum.

When my sister Hazel died, Father also changed. He ended the decades-long feud with Isaiah. Sonny tried to explain what happened. He made it sound like my father broke down and told Isaiah about my sister's death. Isaiah consoled him, and they started conversing, forgetting the bilious feud they'd nurtured for years.

Father didn't admit any friendship with Isaiah. Instead, he quietly accepted that life was larger than their feud. A lifetime pretending that the other did not exist came to a quiet end.

Years later, Sonny's brother Curly cut down the cedar tree under which I stole my first kiss. A truck from the plains came and hauled off the wood to make furniture. By then Isaiah had fallen ill, and his daughter came from the big city and took him to live with her. He would not have allowed anyone to cut down his cedar trees. He built their dark legend and always protected them even as they blocked peering eyes from his private world.

People of my father's and Isaiah's generation grew cedar trees for lumber. They employed sawyer men, such as Mass Harry, to turn the lumber into boards, but they on no occasion sold the timber. Boards were priceless. Their generation used the wood for construction, furniture making, and building coffins to bury their dead. Members of the community collaborated in making the coffins for a deceased love one. As they worked, they told stories, drank rum, and sipped coffee. The ritual helped the men grieve.

When Curly cut the tress, it signaled the passing of an era. People were beginning to send their deceased relatives to the funeral parlor in town. However, the funeral home refused the corpse unless you paid for their expensive, imported coffins. The villagers stopped coming together to build coffins, and cedarwood lost its ceremonial value.

Even though I craved change in our valley, I ached as the legend of the cedar trees died. On moonlit nights, there was never again a shadow for mystery or romance at Isaiah's gate. The lizards forever disappeared from the valley.

My romance with Jasmine exacerbated the conflict of my dual existence. When I saw her in town, I fit in. Back in the hills, I swung an axe as well as any other teen. On weekends, dirt covered me like any other farm boy. Jasmine never saw me on the farm, and I felt she could not understand my humble country life.

Mocho Mountain

The tread of feet through grass,
above the intermittent gusts.
Wind blowing through the long gulley
brings a trace of rotting leaves
and a taste of plowed earth.
Motionless, lonely peaks
sit above dark valleys knee high in shadows.

A bird foraging on the ground
breaks the hush with her call.
She flees to escape the disturbed silence
and Mocho Man treads on softly.

Chapter 64

I walked fearlessly past the dark cemetery where the dead folks from our village lay buried. Sapphire-blue light from Peenie Wallies ducked among the tombstones and then disappeared. The long walks in the dark with my father long ago cured me of any local superstition about ghosts in the cemetery.

Jasmine came to visit her grandmother again, and I arranged to meet her. Her family pressured her to shun me, and for the first time, cracks appeared in our relationship. Our meetings at school were short and tense. *An evening together will fix all that*, I thought as I walked to see her.

I told Ma Rene that I intended to help Jasmine with homework. We spread the books on the table at the back of the house. Ma Rene kept prompting us to hurry up and finish, so I could go home. Neither Jasmine nor I planned to do any homework. We quickly moved to doing what we enjoyed, talking. Suddenly, her grandmother appeared in the room. The shy smile left her face for a scowl.

"Get out of my house!" she yelled, her eyes bright and shining. She pointed the way to the door.

Here in the mountains, I earned most people's respect. Folks often invited me into their homes. Ma Rene and I had previously enjoyed a warm relationship. Her sudden rage caught me off guard, and I responded slowly. She fired again, stepping closer and slamming her foot on the wooden floor. The glassware in the china cabinet rattled her fury.

With a sinking heart, I reached the door and pulled on the bolt that served as a night latch. It refused to budge. Desperately, angrily, I tried again. The door opened, and I stepped outside into the cool, fresh air. All the pent-up emotion of trying to maintain a relationship that nobody wanted to happen broke to the surface.

For most of my life, I did the right things because they were the right things to do. Wrong or right, I wanted this girl for me. Nobody cared. They wanted her too and would do anything to get her.

Suddenly Jasmine's arms were around me, holding me. I struggled to get away from the place that had turned so bitter, but she kept holding on as I sobbed. When I quieted, she let me go, and I stepped into the gloom beyond the house.

Then I heard her voice calling again from behind me. We had used her pen for homework, and it remained pinned to my shirt pocket. I handed it to her, and she held my arm. In the dark, we found each other, and she kissed my lips and found the warm tears flowing. She kissed them away. I could taste the salt mixing with the sweetness from her lips. The tears came harder.

Her grandmother raged again. Through the door, the last bit of light strained to penetrate the night. I pulled away and the darkest night in these hills swallowed me up. The door slammed behind, and the stillness of death joined me on my long walk home. Not even the Peenie Wallies were out as I passed the cemetery. They took their light elsewhere.

Dark hills, solitary witness
share my secrets.
Moaning trees in the wind
speak not my thoughts.

Chapter 65

Jasmine's attendance at school became irregular. On odd days, I could not find her bubbling among the sea of faces. I fully expected to see her every day, and when I didn't, life fell flat. After more than a week of waiting, I caught up with her. She explained that her family took a trip to their home in a secluded Negril Beach area. She thought I shouldn't be upset because I had not seen her for a week. We fought for the first time.

I found some relief from the uncertainties of our relationship by preparing for the annual Sports Day event at my school. I trained with my older friend Will, and based on my performance at training events, I expected to win a medal in the 800-meter race.

The big day arrived, and I did not have Jasmine in my corner. The 800-meter race was one of the first events in the morning, and I lined up at the starting line. After the first lap, we bunched to the inside lane, each man pressing for the lead. I ran well until I felt a piercing stab in my left Achilles heel. My friend Longers, sprinting behind me, had stepped in the back of my leg with his running spikes.

I pressed on, but my leg felt numb, so I pulled out of the race. The physical education teacher watching the turns did not see the accident. Longers went on to win the race. I had beaten him in practice the previous week. I pulled down my socks and found blood oozing from two neat puncture wounds on either side of my Achilles' tendon.

I found the assistant principal and showed her my wounds. She quickly bundled me into her car and took me to the hospital nearby. They gave me an antibiotic shot and scheduled me to return for follow-up shots. Back in the country, they would have wiped a little alcohol on it and sent me on my way. However, I cherished the extra attention to fill the void left by Jasmine's absence.

The assistant principal took me back to be a spectator for the rest of the games. What I saw next made me wish I had gone home to the simple life back in the mountains. Jasmine leaned against the big cotton tree talking to another boy. They were completely isolated from everyone else and absorbed in chatter.

I had seen him before as Jasmine and I walked home from school. The rumormongers claimed he was once her boyfriend. I forgot the pain in my leg for a greater one in my heart.

Fortunately, Larry the class tormentor did not see them chatting, or he easily would have ridiculed me for my failings. No one seemed to notice that Jasmine kept company with someone else. Maybe I cared too much. I sat in the pavilion and pretended to watch the races.

A few older lads from my area came to the sports competition. One of them offered his broad shoulders for me to lean on as I limped to the town center to catch the minivan home. I felt fine enough to walk, but I accepted the chance to pretend my wound, and not my broken spirit, contorted my face. I leaned on his shoulder and limped to town.

In the countryside, not a soul knew about my passionate life in the plains. They were used to seeing me serving as a youth leader in the community and the church. Usually, they bought in on my goody, goody image.

When we got to the square, I got off the minivan without help. Everything felt better as I walked the road up the hill to my house. For the first time in my life, I blessed my dual life. I lived in this remote region away from where status mattered so much. Here I was just one of the sons of the soil. A welcome awaited anyone who failed outside this neighborhood. I felt at home with Abbot and the folks with broken spirits.

At home, the dinner waiting held a special meaning. A mother's unconditional love for her children helped her stay in a bitter marriage. I could not complain about the whims of a wealthy girl in town.

Everyone in my family fought through their own anguish. Mamma hid her pains from the betrayal of love and life. Father fought his demons and summoned his aging muscles to put in another hard day on the farm. My siblings and I fought the reality of living in a dysfunctional family. Most of all, my family never found a way to release the pent-up grief from the untimely passing of my sister.

Nighttime found me seeking relief in writing poetry. I could tell the pages about all my pains without fear of judgment or rebuke. The words flowed out in unbridled sentiments, and by the time I finished writing, the negative emotions drained away from my heart.

On the afternoon of the next day, as I listened to the quiet of the hills, someone called my name. The lad who lived next to Jasmine's grandmother appeared. I was shocked to see him standing before my house with a letter in his hand. He always competed for Jasmine's affections.

He handed me the note and walked away before I could respond. Jasmine had penned my name neatly on the envelope.

I wondered how much Jasmine had paid him to deliver the note. He detested me and might not bring the letter, unless it was a Dear John letter. I toyed with the letter before slowly opening it. Perfume trailed into the air, and drops from a light drizzle blurred the words, but I read that she heard about my injury and felt sorry it happened. Could I come to her grandmother's house?

As soon as the rain subsided, I took to the road. Gone were my injuries to body or spirit. I took the shortcut through the dense woods over rock walls and unpaved paths. In my rush, I scarcely noticed the wet bushes and trees, and, as I passed, they sprinkled me generously. By the time I got to her, the sun slid behind peaks and night crawled in, laying the day to rest.

One call at her door and she reached for me. For an instant, I wondered if she had changed in the weeks that I had not seen her. She fell into my arms, and all my doubts about her love disappeared.

The next day, Sunday, I went to see her again. Of course, I visited her in the evening after church. Nobody went calling during the day. That meant you were without value to your family during the day.

The cool evenings in these mountains fostered the mood for love. Long shadows filled the valleys and tamed the blaze of the sun. Again, I waited for a sun shower to pass before I ventured out. Rainwater added magic to the evening. Light danced from droplets clinging to every twig, and the trees put on a flurry of lush leaves.

As soon as I arrived at her grandmother's, a neighbor told me Jasmine went down the road to visit her a cousin. As I ambled down the hill, Jasmine ran to me. Her cousin gave me the "cut eye" look, as if I were the devil stealing her true love. Everybody wanted Jasmine, and no one wanted to share.

When we walked under the trees, I pulled down a branch laden with rainwater and shook it gently on her. I skipped away and watched her get drenched. She broke out in laughter. Arm in arm, we walked away into the cool evening.

I should have asked her why she did not show up to cheer me on at the sports competition. I ought to have asked her about the ex-boyfriend under the silk cotton tree, but one look in her eyes and I did not care. In her arms, everybody else was far, far away.

Chapter 66

Almost a whole year had passed since I met Jasmine on the minivan. The high school graduating class planned a ball, and I bought tickets for her and me. Her parents would not allow her to attend the ball with me, but she promised to find a way.

I planned to dance with the local princess, so I needed a suit. A tailor in town showed me a catalog depicting the best styles in the United States. Men dressed in suits with multiple pleats and sporting large Afros modeled brightly colored suits.

I purchased the fabric from a store owned by a family of Syrian immigrants. The proprietor showed me the selection of materials. Polyester was the only cloth to choose from, and I picked a sky-blue color. I doubted the tailor could reproduce the lavish designs in the catalog, but I chose the fanciest—I wanted to impress my princess.

One of the girls from my church combed and braided my tight, curly hair two days before the ball. On the big day, I loosened the braids and picked my hair into a full-size Afro. I felt the wind blowing through my Afro, and it evoked a strange yet pleasant sense of freedom.

My tailor delivered, and my three-piece suit was a perfect copy of the one from the catalog. He even reproduced the fancy pleats that adorned the jacket. The teachers transformed a church hall into a ballroom, and our suits and gowns made us lords and ladies. Disco music was king, and my bell-bottomed pants were the perfect size for making an impression on the dance floor.

A band played for a packed dance floor. I waited anxiously for Jasmine, hoping that by some miracle she could make it. My greatest fear was that her mom had locked her in for the night and leave me leaning on the back wall, sweating alone in my blue suit.

My friend Longers waited with me. It felt good to have his company. My other friend, Josie, was missing. His mom had recently passed away, and he stayed home to watch his younger siblings.

The night lit up when Jasmine swept through the door, late as usual. I gasped when I saw her framed against the darkness outside and looking regal in her full-length gown. Her dress flowed around her curves and highlighted her innocent beauty. She looked so adorable tiptoeing in her high-heeled shoes. Her hair fell to her shoulders and surrounded her face with soft wavy curls. It shocked me that she did all this for me.

She scanned the room for me, and for a moment, she seemed so insecure, dressed up and looking grown-up, yet she had to steal away from her mother to my arms. I pulled her into my arms lest she run back out the door and disappear into the night. Even in heels, she tiptoed to reach my lips for a kiss.

"How did you do it?" I gasped, a little out of breath.

She explained that her brother covered for her. They told their parents he was taking her out. We headed for the dance floor. Other couples made space for us and watched as we swirled. You could not really call what we did a dance. We were so close, not even light could come between us. She gave me her purse to hold so she could wrap both arms around me. I stuffed the purse into my pocket, and it lumped up, hard and filled with money. I ignored it and let my hands steal to where her backless dress gave way to skin. Money could not buy what we had, nor could it buy us the time we needed.

When the band took a break, we walked outside under the stars. All the heat from the day had dissipated, and the usually hot, noisy plains fell quiet. The night welcomed us and swallowed us into its belly. In the arms of this most prized daughter of the plains, I made peace with this town that never welcomed me on my daily pilgrimage from the mountain slopes to these halls of learning. When the band resumed, we lingered outside, frozen in the moment.

Back inside, a group of friends called us over, and we swirled together, hoping to stay the night with all its promise and yet keep our innocence too. Beyond this night, a world of adulthood waited, and no one seemed ready to trade the moment for uncertainties.

Jasmine's brother showed up too soon to drive her home. I cursed him for coming back so quickly. *Had he no girl*? As she fled to his Toyota pickup, she glanced back at me longingly, and then she transformed into the little girl her mother wanted her to be. She slammed the door shut. Her brother gunned the engine, and they raced off with the headlights probing the uncertain night.

I wandered back to the dance floor to listen to the band. The memory of Jasmine's voice, her smell, her warm body filled the place, and I made light of the rest of the night. The band played the last song, covering a song made famous by an American pop singer.

The singer's baritone was full of sadness, and he masked all traces of his Jamaican accent. I stood a step away from the stage and sang my heart out.

"In your arms, I can only feel love again."

As I sang the final note, I dropped to my knees, empty hands reaching for lost love. The crescendo of the drums ceased. In silence, the light flickered on before I could stand. Laughter welcomed me back.

"Manny on his knees singing."

Longers led the laughter. Perhaps he felt embarrassed to see his friend humbled on his knees. I shrugged it off. What did he know about "in your arms I can only feel love again?" He had come to the ball alone.

Chapter 67

The following summer, my father paid me for labor normally performed by a farm hand. I convinced him I could do the annual summer cleaning of the citrus groves at my Aunt Edith's house.

My aunt moved out to live with my Uncle Buster after Uncle Mack died. She took care of Buster since he lost a leg to diabetes-related complications. Her brightly colored house remained unoccupied, but the citrus groves still needed attention. My father took over the duties on her farm.

Father usually employed young men who dropped out of school for farm work. These youth's skills with a machete were superior to mine, but they were my age, and I felt I could do the work as well. I asked some of my friends from my church youth group to join me at the task. They jumped at the thought of making extra money.

The job required some skill with a machete. We could not hoe the weed because we might damage the delicate roots and ruin next season's citrus crop. To do the job correctly, I squatted, slid the machete's blade under the roots of the weeds, and pulled the weeds. Next, I shook off the soil and then tossed the weeds into a compost pile under each tree.

I slid the machete as quickly as I could, but I still fell behind my companions. Will, my friend from many adventures, worked furiously ahead of the pack. Out on summer break from the university, he discarded his intellectual mindset and worked like a common laborer.

Andy, another of my friends, toiled ahead of me. He was a city boy, but hard times and a lifelong dispute with his dad forced him back to the mountains. He sometimes clashed with country folks, but I loved his sense of adventure.

Andy followed us to church to get together with Merle, one of Will's sisters. He managed for a while, but lately he fell out of favor with her. Andy thought my father's frequent prodding about his work ethic meant that Father disliked him, but my father only spoke to people he liked.

Father came to check on us periodically and left without comment. This meant we were doing all right. I had chosen some fine young men to work with me.

At the end of the day, I washed off as much of the dirt as possible and then went to the crossroad to watch whatever entertainment the locals mustered up. Alonzo, the saxophone player whose wife left for England, still waited for her return nearly two decades later. He never played the saxophone again, and he fell out of favor with the younger generation who knew nothing of his musical talent.

I met Will and his girlfriend, Sheila. She, like me, was closing out the teenage years. Her family and mine maintained a very close friendship for many years. Sheila stood almost as tall as Will. Her feet barely touched the ground as they strolled through the village square.

Will and Sheila wanted to spend the night together, so I offered to get the key for Aunt Edith's unoccupied house. We all planned to stay in the house and have an early start on the work in the citrus groove.

Father left the keys to Aunt Edith's house unattended on a table at home. Only he had access to the house, and no one considered challenging his authority. Stealthily, I pocketed the keys and slipped out to meet Will, Sheila, and Andy. On my way, I took a few of the eggs Mamma collected from the fowl coop. I pretended Father gave me the key and his approval to bring friends to Aunt Edith's house.

At the grocer, we bought supplies for next morning's breakfast and then strolled to Aunt Edith's house. I used the key to open the back door and proceeded to open the inner door to the bedrooms. The door refused to budge. We all took turns, but the lock remained steadfast. Sheila shifted uncomfortably and glanced away.

"We'll break the lock," I offered.

"Are you sure Uncle Gil won't kill you?" Andy inquired cautiously.

He knew my father's legend as a tough, hard-driving man. Father had little bite left, but he barked to defend his reputed vigor. I refused their caution, and we braced and carefully bent the lock mechanism enough to push the door open. Will and Sheila went to the larger room. Andy and I shared the smaller back room with the twin beds.

Before going to sleep, I wondered what Jasmine might be doing down on the hot plains. I hadn't seen her since we'd gotten out of school for the summer. Her mother kept her tightly guarded in their store in town. Tired from the day's work, I fell asleep.

A trail of fog lifted from dew-drenched grass when we rose next morning. Sheila busied herself fixing breakfast while we sharpened our machetes like grown men. Soon smoke rose from the fire, and the eggs sizzled in the pan. The smell of fried ripe plantains replaced the freshness of the mountain air.

Andy handed me a plate and pointed to the crest of the hill.

"Uncle Gil a come."

Father's upper body was just visible, as he headed in our direction. He always walked swiftly. He carried the bamboo cane I wanted him to discard when we bid farewell to Cousin Cedric. Father used the cane sparingly, and it never slowed him down.

In a few minutes, he would round the horseshoe bend and set on us. We wanted to enjoy a breakfast of fried plantains, scrambled eggs, and sourdough bread. Folks normally sipped a cup of mint tea to begin the day, but we swallowed ours.

Sheila washed dishes, and we held our tools ready for the fields as Father stormed in. I got these boys into trouble, and I had to do the explaining. He looked us over and acknowledged Sheila. He loved her family. He nodded to Will. Everyone knew Will's leadership in the community. He held his judgment on Andy. I waited for him, unsure what form my punishment might take.

"Gimme the keys," he said in a surprisingly calm voice.

I handed them to him quickly. He hated to repeat himself. God knows he certainly spoke loud enough for the deaf to hear. He took the keys without looking at me and headed for the broken door.

Sheila finished the dishes; we stepped quickly out of the kitchen and walked across the dew-drenched fields to the citrus groves. I listened for his call, a thunderous "Dan-Dan," but it never came. Silently we marched to the fields and bent our backs to the task.

When we came back to my aunt's house for lunch, Father had already left, but he'd fixed the broken lock before he departed. It took us a whole week to clear the weeds in the citrus grove. All the time I waited for Father's fury to be unleashed on me for breaking into my aunt's house.

On Friday, Father came early with the money for our labor. He gave me the bills and left without comment. I got away with something my father's reputation never should have allowed. Somehow, I figured out how to balance my goody-goody role with my mischievous side.

I paid my friends and went home to scrub my hands free of the chlorophyll stains from a week of pulling at the weeds. No amount of scrubbing could get rid of the calluses on my hand, so I washed them as best as I could and hoped Jasmine would ignore them. Tomorrow was Saturday, and I planned to visit her home while her parents were at work.

Chapter 68

On Saturday mornings, I liked to take the long walk to harvest sweet potatoes from Shell's farm plot back in the woods. For years, Shell asked me to take the trip with him. I refused. I could not think of anything back in the woods that appealed to me.

Moreover, his brother was Rooster — the man with the wandering eye — and his sisters ran the gang that bullied Father. Shell had long ago broken company with his wayward relatives, but the stigma of his family endured. At eighteen, I could balance the contradiction of his heritage and his more jovial personality. I finally decided to take the trip to his farm lot.

To get to his farm, we climbed a trail that meandered up a steep hillside. For most of the walk, we were under a canopy of tropical hardwood trees, but at the top, the path opened to let light in. I looked back down the slopes and fought hard the temptation to glide with the hawks across the trees to the valley floor.

Uncle Mack's home perched next to Salaman's giant silk cotton tree. Aunt Edith painted the house in bright, happy colors. Any day, the bauxite company would displace her and mine the land.

Next to the tree, a small grocery shop waited for customers. Father bought our supplies there on Saturdays, since he no longer needed to take time to chop wood for fuel. That was my job.

A dusty, unpaved road ran a winding path through the valley. The road lost its way among the trees as it climbed up the slopes and exited. In the morning, the country bus ran the route, taking women to sell their produce in the town. In the evening, it lumbered back to bring them home. On Fridays, the bread delivery van came through to stock up the shops for the weekend. It then fled ahead of a small cloud of red dust. At this time of day, no vehicles were taking the turns below.

In the valley, a woman leading a donkey laden with produce marched through. Not a single soul ever called out across the gap to this sacred place. The climb brought you in communion with a profound stillness. You did not speak, lest you shatter the moment. Down there, people were toiling.

Shell and I hiked down the other side of the hill, through more trees, and to another opening. Off to the side of the hill, Shell grew banana trees, and he let some of the fruit ripen on the tree. This was one reason I loved to take this long walk back through the woods. Nothing tasted better than tree-ripened bananas. He watched as I shook the tree and the fruits fell into my hand like fingers of gold. They were too ripe to be carried back home and too cloying to be eaten in large quantities. We just ate a few and moved on.

Beyond more trees and into another clearing, we came face to face with the main reason I made the trip. A field of sweet potatoes, the vines and leaves a sea of purple and green, waited. Nestled in the cool earth beneath the vines, the crop waited for the harvest.

"Slargs," Shell called the large, heavy sweet potatoes. I think he meant to say 'its large' like he might have heard from an educated man. Shell often made up terms when the local Patois had no word for a situation. To avoid ruining the poetry of the moment, I just accepted his construction of the term.

I took home some of the slargs to Mamma, and she made the sweet potato pudding everyone craved. When the puddings were cooled, Shell could have his cut. He only wanted a wedge. Like the ripened bananas, eating too much was worse than having none at all.

I gave no thought to my favorite Saturday morning activities as I left home to meet Jasmine at her house. Her letters told me her father's schedule and when I could visit safely. She explained in detail how to get to her home. Her father built the house from a Chinese pagoda design. She also told me to watch for the tall Norfolk Island pine tree that framed the attic.

When I got to her house, she took me to the secluded attic. It was a private bedroom where a guest might stay or where a family member might go for some solitude. In our isolation, we explored our pent-up emotions. We lost our innocence amidst the uncertain mixture of light from the window filtering through the shadows from the tall pine tree swaying in the wind.

I took the ride back home, pondering the strange calm that sedated my body. The people on the minivan sat contemplating their own thoughts and left me alone to live in my moment. My feet touched the ground lightly when the van arrived at the crossroad. I walked home suppressing the feeling that my life just took a profound turn. I could not wait for the summer to be over, so I could rekindle my romance with Jasmine at school.

Chapter 69

Over the summer, the letters stopped coming, so I went to see Jasmine at her family store in town. Her mother, Mrs. Singh, frowned from behind the tall counter. She seemed to be expecting me. For the first time, I saw her up close. Her eyes were oval-shaped like Jasmine's, only flashing anger.

I asked to see Jasmine, and she glared at me as if I were dirt—red dirt on her spotless floor. The boy who studied at night by the pale glare of a kerosene lamp pleaded to speak to the daughter of the family with the largest store in town.

She walked toward me, trying to intimidate me. Her hand pawed the latest electric desk lamp, miming *mine, mine*.

My family used kerosene lamps. Nobody in my neighborhood had electricity or appliances. If she sold kerosene oil, donkey rope or machetes, this would be my kind of place.

"I heard you came to my house. What were you doing there?"

I hunted for an answer, and she fired again.

"Don't you know that Mr. Singh will shoot you?"

Her hands caressed the television sets she had on sale.

No sound came out of my open mouth.

Mr. Singh, Jasmine's father, had shot a boy at their home. I did not take her threat lightly. Powerful people get away with murder in this town. Her eyes narrowed, hunting my face for weakness. Seemingly, she found it and huffed, dismissing me as if I were dust of a moth puffed on the wind.

Jasmine saved the day. She ran from the back of the store and took my hand. We endured her mother saying, "You can't talk here in my place of business." The woman kept raising her voice, so we cut our conversation. I dismissed her rants. School will resume in a week, and I would have my girl all to myself.

A few weeks later as I rode the minivan home from school, it stopped at the junction at Cedars to pick up passengers for the last leg of our trip. I clutched a letter from Jasmine in my shirt pocket and pretended to be asleep.

"What is wrong, Manny?" an older lad from the village asked.

"My stomach hurts," I lied.

"Come," he offered. "Let me buy you a drink. It will mek your belly feel better."

I never drank alcohol, but better to drink than to reveal the true cause of my pain. I kept quiet about the letter in my pocket. We got off the van and walked to the rum bar. Men, like Abbot, nursing secret pains with alcohol shifted their elbows and made room at the bar. They nodded a welcome as the promising boy scholar and his companion joined them to drink in defeat.

"Two gin and water," my lad ordered.

He handed the glass with the clear fluid sitting lifelessly on the bottom. The gin burned my throat on its way down and dropped into the void at the pit of my stomach. The other men fixated on their drinks.

A year earlier, I ran with Will for six-miles from this same spot to the village square. Back then, I scoffed at the drunks with whom I now rubbed shoulders.

I touched the Dear John letter in my pocket. Jasmine promised to return to school at the end of the long summer that kept us apart. Classes resumed, and she never appeared among the sea of faces at school. She did not reply to my letters, so I tracked down her best friend.

The girl stared me down with dark, distant eyes and refused to say a word. She surpassed her reputation for reticence. I resisted the temptation to shake an answer out of her, but I walked away like a ghost.

The next day, the best friend told me Jasmine wanted me to return all her letters and poems. The passion of our relationship always shone brightly in our poems to each other. Perplexed, I packed them and handed them over to her friend. Maybe this would cause her to rethink her decision to stay away from me. No such thing happened.

A few days later, she sent the Dear John letter now hiding in my breast pocket. No perfume touched the edges of the pages. Bitter blame filled every word, pointing a long finger at me for causing her pain. What had she experienced after we left each other? What made her change mind about us? Why didn't she tell me anything?

"Feel better?" Back in the minivan, the lad probed again.

The heat from the drink went to a different place than my pain. It did nothing to abate my angst. My aches ran deeper.

"Yes," I lied, faking a smile.

The successful scholar who traveled daily to the best school in town was almost home. The youth leader could not show his cracked ego. I pulled myself together. Big men don't cry.

Now I could go home and bleed through my pen. Poetry gutted the low feeling in my stomach, filing it away in a safe place. I vented my pain on paper without being ashamed because my girl had left me. Anyway, no one understood me except my friend Will, but he lived far away at the university in the big city. Just because it made me feel better, I wrote him a letter, but never mailed it.

Chapter 70

The last time I saw Jasmine, she was going to see her grandma. She looked past me and took another seat. Her contempt stilled the air. I could not understand how someone so warm could now turn as cold as the north winds. Her letters held so much poison that I knew she must hate me. Fortunately, not a soul in the minivan seemed to know about our romance, or her scorn would have headlined Abbot's sermons at the crossroad.

On a piece of paper, I scribbled a poem to her about starting over. *Yes,* I thought, *after she reads this, I will be back with her*. My poems could turn even a heart of stone. Jasmine folded the paper without reading it and looked at me like I was dust of a moth, puffed to the wind.

Numb inside, I waited for my poetry to work its usual magic. I feared she might turn around and shout that she'd *left me*.

As I waited for her answer, I realized we'd taken this same ride before. We were in this same minivan when I first saw her more than a year before. The same sullen Rasta man drove the van.

The minivan stopped at her grandmother's house, and she hopped out. She had cut her hair short and pulled it back tight, showing her strained features. For the first time, I saw the pointy ear she always concealed with her hair. She was still flawless.

Her sky-blue dress made her look much younger than her eighteen years. My heart never danced as it did when I first saw her cross the lawn. I wondered how all the excitement turned to a lump in my chest. She left without saying good-bye.

> I left my heart staked like a shadow
> where it fell when it broke.
> I've built so many mounds
> behind which to hide,
> so that in looking back
> I would not see me there
> weeping and bleeding.

> Walking back past time measured
> in forgotten faces,
> and tastes of different lands,
> through perfumes and sweat,
> to teenaged pages left unread,
> now turned yellow.
> Unwittingly opening old wounds
> left unhealed,
> I find my heart buried with teenage dreams.

As Jasmine left me, I added up the hours spent traveling to and from school. I thought of Gina, the girl on the bus with the empty seat waiting for me. Over the years, months of my life had passed in transit. I formed relationships that only existed on a moving vehicle

I never saw Gina again. The young woman whose soft allure made a magic ride out of the dusty bus trip left my life journey. I could never face her after I saw her pained expression framed in the bus window. Though she lived in the next village, we never again crossed paths. Perhaps she returned to her native Saint Mary, on the other side of the island where the rain fell daily.

The Rasta man watched me in the rearview mirror of the minivan. A rare smile cracked his masked face. He waited a little longer than usual before slowly pulling away from the curb. A deafening silence filled the van. I wiped my sweaty palms on my trousers.

Later, someone mentioned that Jasmine's mom shipped her off to live with relatives in the United States. I went cold inside.

Chapter 71

Mamma fixed her gaze on the American airlines plane on the tarmac. My sister Jan climbed gracefully up the stairs and never glanced back at us in the waving gallery. She bowed her head, pretending to concentrate on each step. At the last stair, she turned, and her eyes swept over us. Her wave closed a chapter of our lives. I could not see the tears that must have filled her eyes.

For the first time in my life, Mamma seemed helpless. Her face fell apart as she cried. Always an antidote to Father's harsh personality, she knew how to soften every blow of life. Now she struggled for the right words to express her feelings. At some subconscious level, we all felt this was a final good-bye to her only remaining daughter.

I placed my hands around her shoulders and kissed her on the cheek. I was shocked by how soft her face felt, as if it was about to turn into mush. She seemed confused by my kiss. Unable to voice her uncertainty, she rebuked sternly instead.

"You don't know about kissing until you go abroad."

I remained silent. Finding the right words to comfort a parent is nigh impossible. When my sister passed away only Braman knew the right words to comfort Mamma.

"Can a mother's tender care cease towards the child she bears," he offered as his eyes twinkled. She forced a smile for him.

Mamma cared for us deeply, but never showed affection by kissing. Foreigners, of course, openly showed their emotions when they visited. Mamma, though, showed her unwavering love by touching, grooming, baking, or working long hours to make our lives bearable.

I kept my hand around her shoulder as I contemplated the implications of her prediction to "go abroad." *Did this mean that I, too, would one day mount the steps of an airplane to "go abroad?"* My brother Serge pulled closer, feeling for warmth from a family often broken by tragedy, bitter arguments, and now the departure of our sister.

After Jan left to live in New York, I moved to Kingston, the big city, to work with the Library Service. While in the city, I followed the crowds to the National Stadium to pay final respects to the Reggae star, Knotty. People piled their bodies toward the door of the stadium and struggled to catch a glimpse of his remains. The artist's songs played softly over the speakers in the stadium. His rusty tenor almost cracked with the pain of his message as he sang. Knotty gave his life to articulating the emotions of the common person. Now his songs rang out his own eulogy.

> In an island, so full of sun
> some people only know the rain.
> My world is covered in darkness,
> I say …

Without warning, a man in military fatigues lifted his rifle and fired a canister of tear gas to keep the masses at bay. The crowd broke like waves spilling on the beach. A foreign photographer, undaunted by the fumes, rushed forward to snap pictures of the panic on people's faces. I pictured news headlines in Europe and America: "Natives Riot at Funeral of Reggae Star." There must be a better way to send a fallen hero on his long journey where travelers go and never send back a message.

I squeezed into the arena to join the folks filing past the coffin. The coffin seemed too large for Knotty's helpless face, but he was more message than man. A spirit that captured sayings of the common person and turned them into anthems could never fit in a coffin. His song blaring on the loud speakers predicted the mood of the day.

"Where is the sun in my world today?"

The week before Knotty died, my father, an unheralded hero passed away in our village. I returned to the hills to take our last walk. He had made it through the night, past the predawn "red cloud," and departed quietly in his bed. Mornings were always his favorite time.

He asked for me before his death, but I lived fifty miles away in Kingston. When I got the news of his death, I felt nothing except the need to rush to see his remains before they took him off to the mortuary.

At home, Mamma held her emotions back during the days before the funeral. People flooded our house to pay their last respects. They came in trickles during the day and in droves at night. A few of the neighbors came to clean, chop wood, or even cook; but the major burden of hosting fell on Mamma, Serge, and me.

Some of the visitors wanted to have a "singing wake," and I tried to convince them my family traditions prohibited singing during the time of mourning. Several times they broke out in songs, and they didn't stop until Mamma pleaded wearily that she needed rest. I put an end to the singing and sent them home.

We still kept cedar boards stacked neatly under the cellar of the house. However, the tradition of the community coming together and making a casket had ended. We had to buy a coffin from the funeral home.

Mamma showed very little sign of the strain, except that she seemed willing to turn over decisions to me. Some of the duties I accepted with reluctance, and others I relished. At the funeral service, I stood next to Mamma as she gave a loud cry and slumped a little. I embraced her shoulder. She leaned ever so slightly toward me. After that, Mamma was never the same.

My father's death affected her in the most unusual way. I thought his passing might free her to express the many creative talents she'd stifled during her decades of marriage. Instead, she experienced what I later learned was a nervous breakdown. In backward, rural Jamaica, the primitive medical system never diagnosed or treated her condition.

My older brother Phil, who became Mamma's financial supporter, confessed to me that Mamma had been receiving cancer treatment for nearly ten years. All through my early teens, she traveled to Kingston to get radiation treatment for what the doctor told her was a "growth." Her long, wavy hair gradually thinned, and she hated the nausea from the treatments.

The doctors refused to tell her she had cancer, lest she worry herself to death. Our older siblings refused to tell Serge or me. Mamma slowly wasted away from the radiation, and the "growth" gradually took over her body.

I felt a deep sadness for Mamma as another door on her happiness closed. She gave every bit of her energy to "see us past the worst." We would have to live for the joy life journey denied her.

Father's death took the vitality out of the valley below our house. Silence replaced the sound of his machete chopping wood and the crunching of pebbles as he charged around tending his crops. Even the fruit trees lost some of their will to produce. Nobody else could coax life from the rocky soil as he could.

Chapter 72

A year after Father's death, I went to say good-bye to Mamma. I planned to leave for New York the next day and attend my sister Jan's wedding. By then, Mamma had returned to her childhood community. I usually visited her several times a month, ferrying groceries or money from my older brother Phil. Mamma seemed content in the village of her childhood.

She was supposed to make some of her sweet potato puddings for me to take to Jan, but they were not ready. I lost my patience with her. I planned to return quickly to the city and pack for my departure to New York.

"See you look like your father," she vented.
I heard, "You are impatient like your father."

Comparing me to Father's abrupt manner brought up the burden of sucking sour grapes. I preferred Mamma's calm personality as opposed to Father's abrupt style, so I sat and pretended to be calm until she finished baking.

Mamma and I rarely quarreled, and I wished she'd just say *walk good,* blessing my journey. Our argument distracted us from the fear we both felt at this uncertain junction in the road.

It surprised me that my plans to leave disturbed her. Maybe she had come to rely on me for some sort of consistency in her life. My father, the great provider, left big shoes for me to fill. Perhaps she felt I would never return to live in Jamaica. Everyone who got the slightest chance left the island so bereft of opportunities, but I planned to return in three weeks.

As I walked away with the basket laden with the puddings, I had my own lucid premonition. Never again would I see her in the little cottage by the sweet potato fields. I am sure she felt it too. Mamma possessed a keen intuition for unfolding events. Neither of us found the words to confront the uneasy feeling.

Mamma looked so vulnerable. Back when the inspector had proclaimed that I *will go far in life*, she held me close and saw me through the storms of my life. Now at her most uncertain crossroad, I must leave. If I were not so schooled in stifling my feelings, I would be crying.

In her earlier years, Mamma was the sweetest person in the world. Unlike my father, she showed infinite patience to everyone. With impeccable timing, she knew when to pull the charcoal from beneath the sweet potato pudding and bake the most delicious morsel on earth.

When we were little, the smell of the pudding taunted us all evening as it cooled on top of the cabinet in the living room. Mama told Serge and me to wait until the morning to cut the pudding when it had cooled. We never waited.

While our parents slept, we sliced a wedge and sat at the dining table to relish the sweetness and the perfect blend of spices. Outside the crickets chirped without ceasing, and life tasted sweet. I found out later that our parents were still awake, listening as we chomped away.

Chapter 73

Air Jamaica's Boeing 727 raced across the tarmac, and swift to the winds, it lifted to the skies. For the fraction of a second it took the craft to catch the wind, a tiny pulse of silence rippled through the cabin. In the luggage compartment above my head, my basket filled with sweet potato puddings shifted, and then it settled back in place.

The basket was woven in the traditional *bankra* style of the indigenous people, and their culture predated western colonialism. I carried the artifact of my provincial existence on the long journey to New York, the hub of modern culture. My sister Jan waited for me there. I had not seen her in four years. The airplane leveled off, turned north, and flew back over the lush island. Below me, my mountain home seemed far too small and insignificant to have held so many memories.

Patches of red earth appeared amid the greenery. The mining company had stripped parts of the countryside to get at the underlying bauxite ore. They dug up the land that sustained my family and shipped it off to make beer and soda cans. Bulldozers already mined Thatch Walk, where I had walked secret paths with my father up to the village of Mountain. The earthmovers destroyed the trails leaving behind cavernous mine pits that scarred the landscape.

The smell of the sweet potato pudding permeated the airplane. Mamma had painstakingly baked them in the house by the fields. I settled back for my first flight on an airplane. In a few minutes, the island disappeared into the wide-open Caribbean Sea.

Golden light from the evening sun stayed with us much longer than it should have. The dying glow reflected off a woman's mirror in the seat beside me. She puckered her mouth and applied a plum-colored lipstick.

She caught me staring at her and smiled. Before she could put the mirror away, I glimpsed my reflection. A face like my father's face stared back at me. Except for the worry lines, I looked a lot like him. Was I really driven like him?

I returned her smile and we chatted while the plane sped into the northern skies. She was headed for Mount Vernon, a town north of New York City. I never heard of it and would probably never see her again.

Slowly the sun lost its glow on the western horizon. The lights of New York City appeared below. Life pulsated from every building. My sister, Jan, waited for me down there among the many lights. I had a lot to tell her.

With barely a whisper from the tires, the pilot set the aircraft down on John F. Kennedy International Airport's runway. The passengers broke out in spontaneous applause. Air Jamaica's pilots took pride in pleasing their commuters with a soft landing. My basket in the rack above my seat barely shifted. My sweet potato puddings were safe.

About the Author

Dwight Marshalleck holds a Bachelor of Science from Cornell University, and a Master of Science Education from CUNY Lehman. Born in the bauxite-rich hills of Jamaica, his writing is infused with the imagery and voices of everyday folks.

Dwight's upcoming book ventures into the seductive world of New York urban culture. In addition, he is preparing to launch a musical interpretation of one of Jamaica's most treasured legends.

As a career long science teacher, Dwight invokes his literary twists to augment the lessons and delight his students. He is an avid gardener, and an off-road cyclist, but he still finds time to volunteer for many civic organizations. He lives with his family in Florida.

13695670R00193

Printed in Germany
by Amazon Distribution
GmbH, Leipzig